ARMELLE AKELE

Break the Silence

Overcome fear of judgment by telling your story

Unless otherwise indicated, all scriptures quotations are taken from *The English Standard Version* (ESV) and *The Challenge Study Bible: Celebrating Life Transformation.* Used with permission.

The English Standard Version, copyright @ 2012 by Crossway

The Challenge Study Bible: Celebrating Life Transformation, copyright @ 2019 by Don Wilkerson

To my parents, Gabriel and Albertine Ntougou, for their support and guidance in shaping me into the strong woman I am today. Your absence will be felt forever.

CONTENTS

Prologue

May God receive all the glory as I share
our stories.

~ Armelle Akele

PROLOGUE

Today, after exactly seven years and one day of marriage, I still do not know happiness and peace in my home.

Some things take a toll on you and make you stronger; others affect and weaken you. This weakness results from the intensity of the pain that gnaws at you inside. When grief and pain come together, their result can harm your life. At this point, you cannot pretend; sadness is the only option.

I couldn't pretend because I was in pain. I had turned to prayer, but my prayer to God was empty because I constantly had my misfortune in mind. So, I took my computer and played a praise song, but I had difficulty letting this beautiful melody fill my heart. All my efforts to have inner peace ended up in failure. Not knowing what to do, I decided to go to bed.

Lying on my bed in the darkness of the night, I dwelled on this physical and moral pain that consumed me. The contempt and domestic violence were nothing new; I was used to this treatment. The only difference was that this time, I felt like my body was getting weaker by the day. I had to decide; otherwise, this man could kill me one day. I then asked God: "Why so much contempt for a loved one? Lord, why so much pain?"

The Lord answered me this: "I, *too, have been despised to this day; I continue to be despised by many of you. Still, that doesn't stop me from responding when someone cries out to me. If the one who gives you the breath of life was despised, how could it be any different with you? We must forgive and move on because the best is yet to come. Know that whatever trial you face, I have given you the capacity and the strength to overcome it."*

These words resonated strongly in my heart. It was as if the Lord was speaking to me audibly. Immersed in the darkness of my room, I could feel His light illuminating my heart. If God says we have the strength to face any difficulty, we must believe He is telling the truth because He is God, the Creator of everything. He knows us better than ourselves.

It is essential to learn to depend entirely on God by relying on His word because it has the power to transform our lives. To know who you are and to have the answer to your problem, you need testimonials from people who have found themselves in the same situation and who have overcome it so that they can share their experiences and teach you how they were able to find a way out. To achieve that, you have only one thing to do: open your Bible and ask the Holy Spirit to help and guide you through meditation.

Jesus Christ is the answer to our sorrows. He answered me and got me out of the darkness I was in. This book is my thanksgiving to God for all He has done for me. I would never have been the person I am today without His divine intervention. With God, I can face tomorrow; He holds my future.

The Bible says that all who trust in Him will never be confounded. So, I hold this word in my heart, and I do one thing: *forgetting what lies behind and straining forward to what lies ahead,* I run towards my destiny to accomplish the purpose for which God sent me on earth (Philippians *3:13).* Indeed, by walking according to God's plan for my life and by remaining in obedience to His word, I will be able *to win the prize of the upward call of God in Christ Jesus* (Philippians *3:14).* Therefore, nothing and no one should prevent me from winning this prize.

The trials I face today should not prevent me from accomplishing God's plans. I must be strong and rely on the Lord. It is true that today:

I feel lost and humiliated; thinking about it is a bitter poison. I can't forget anything about it, and I'm overwhelmed. But here's what I want to remember, here's my reason for hope: The steadfast love of the lord never ceases, his mercies never come to an end, they are new every morning. How great is Your faithfulness. The Lord is my treasure, that is why I put my hope in Him. The Lord is good for those who rely on Him, for those who turn to Him. It is good to silently hope for the deliverance the Lord will send (Lamentations 3:19-26).

Thank you, Lord, for the deliverance You will bring in my life. I will keep silent and wait for You by keeping the faith because *I believe that the present sufferings are not worth comparing with the glory that will be revealed in me* (Romans 8:18). Therefore, I know that tomorrow I will witness the manifestation of this deliverance and the renewal of His mercy in my life.

This book is a living testimony to the authenticity and power of the word of God. There is no problem in this world that does not find a solution in the Word of God. The word of God is the answer to the evils of this world. In times of happiness or sorrow, every one of us should turn to the word of God for comfort; it is worthy of praise. We must all take seriously this command that the Lord gave to Joshua because our success on earth and our eternal life depend on it:

This book of the law shall not depart from your mouth, but you shall meditate on it day and night, so that you may be careful to do according to all that is written in it. For then you will make your way prosperous, and then you will have good success (Joshua 1:8). May the Lord help us all to obey this word to win the prize of God's heavenly calling in Jesus Christ and to have a fulfilled life on earth.

1

Learn to Forgive

"Forgive us our wrongs, as we also forgive those who
have wronged us."
~ Matthew 6:12

Clara's letter

*When I was a child, from the age of eight to twelve, my
father's younger brother, who lived with us at the
time, abused me on several occasions. My parents
often left me in his care, and he took advantage of
these moments to rape me. I was still a child, and at
that age, I didn't understand what sexuality was. I
was scared. I didn't know what to think or what to do.*

*He was twenty-two, and I was eight. He threatened to
kill me every time if I told anyone. I was in great pain,
not only because of the atrocity of the act but also*

1

because of the weight of his body on mine because I was only a child. Sometimes I had trouble breathing while he was on top of me. Today, I am twenty-three years old and full of anger and hatred. My uncle in question died four years ago. Yet, I cannot forgive him for all the harm he did to me in my youth, even though he is dead. He ruined part of my childhood.

Two weeks before his death, he called me to apologize because he said he was now a little girl's father and realized what he had done to me was wrong. I replied that it was too late, that I would never forgive him, and that I only wanted one thing: that he died. A few days after his call, his wife found him dead in the bathroom. He had committed suicide. I never confessed this to my family. I have only one desire: to find a way to forgive him and finally have peace. I'm tired of this anger I've been dragging around for years.

CLARA.

Clara wants to free herself from her anger and move on instead of being a prisoner of this feeling that gnaws at her. She knows what she went through was not right. Her past is very painful. Yet, despite everything, she tries to forgive. She knows that it is by forgiving that she will have peace.

We can never say it enough: we must forgive if we want to be forgiven. It is the law of reciprocity. I do something because I would have liked it to be done for me if I were in the same situation. Whatever the wrong, we must forgive. There are wrongs that we can never forget; they can happen. However, no wrong in this world cannot be forgiven. The unforgivable does not exist. Forgiveness exists in any situation, regardless of the suffering. It is difficult and painful to think about, but it will not justify us to the Lord our God.

It is essential to know that the Lord will not judge us for the evil done to us but for how we respond to it. It is our actions that interest God, not those of others towards us. The Lord will not let us give excuses for our conduct. You will not have the right to pronounce sentences like: "Lord, it is because she did this to me that I acted this way. I had no choice but to be like that. Look what I suffered; it was because of this situation that I became wicked." Let God do justice for us. He asks us to forgive so He can take charge of our situation.

Refusing to forgive is taking justice into your own hands; God cannot act if we think we have control over the situation. He only works when we put everything into His hands. We must never forget that God will forgive us if we forgive others. After being nailed to the cross in a terrible state of suffering, Jesus Christ our Savior made this request to God: *"Father, forgive them, for they do not know what they are doing"* (Luke

3

23: 34). If we read the entire Bible from Genesis to Revelation, we will notice that there is not a thing the Lord asks us to do that He did not do Himself. If you pay attention to what is happening around you, you will see that others have experienced the same thing, sometimes even worse. If Jesus Christ forgave those who hurt Him, we too can do it, and we must do it.

Let's stop reading for a moment and think about every time we asked God to forgive us for a sin we committed or the times we offended a loved one, and that person forgave us. No, do not say that these were not serious things or sins because only the person who suffers the offense can determine the extent or gravity of the act committed. No one can affirm that, in his whole life, he has never been forgiven. If such a person exists, it means that this person has never sinned, which is impossible since we are born sinners, and the Bible declares *that there is no righteous man, not even one.* (Romans 3:10)

You see, none of us can claim to be perfect. Only God is perfect. Therefore, we must seek to have the character traits of the One who is excellent. Let us obey His word because He knows what suits our life. The Bible teaches this in Psalm 103, verses 8-10: *The Lord is compassionate and gracious, slow to anger, and abounding in love. He will not always accuse, nor will he harbor his anger forever. He does not treat us as our sins deserve or repay us according to our iniquities.*

See how often the Lord is kind to us despite our faults. Verse 12 of this same chapter tells us: *As far as the east is from the west, so far has he removed our transgressions from us.* Isn't it wonderful to hear such a word? This means that even before we asked Him to forgive us, He had already forgotten our sins. This is what the reference to distance in this biblical passage explains. This distance God places between us and our faults ensures that He does not make us pay the price for our errors. If we had to give a name to this distance, we would call it "forgiveness."

Someone said that refusing to forgive or even hating our fellow human being is like drinking poison and expecting it to kill the person you blame. Not forgiving, if we are not careful, will destroy us, not the person who hurt us. It destroys us little by little, ruins our lives, and blinds us because we tell ourselves that we are right to act in a certain way. However, know that there is always a solution. Often, it is not very far from the feeling that drives us. If it is true that this evil gnaws at you, it is also true that if you decide to forgive, you will be delivered from a great sin, even from several evils. The process can be long, but don't be discouraged. Pray and ask for the help of the Holy Spirit. The Lord will give you the grace to be freed from this feeling of hatred. By accepting to forgive, God will fill your life with peace and happiness.

Before finishing this part, I urge those who do not like

to forgive to change their behavior. If you hurt someone, no matter who he is, ask them for forgiveness. Let's never forget this: everything we do to others, be it good or bad, we do it to ourselves. Forgiveness is paramount, whether you are the offended person or the offender. No one can be born again in Christ unless he asks for forgiveness. Faith in God begins with the forgiveness of sins. Our Lord can forgive only those who ask Him for forgiveness.

My dear Clara,

"Commit your life to the Lord. Trust in Him, and He will act.
Refrain from anger and forsake wrath. Fret not yourself, it tends only to evil. For the evildoers shall be cut off, but those who wait for the Lord shall inherit the land." (Psalm 37:5-11)

Forgiveness, you see, is not something we do for others. We do it for ourselves to be liberated and move forward.

May the Lord our God cover you with His divine peace.

2

The Spirit of God

"There shall come forth a shoot from the stump of
Jesse, and a branch from his roots shall bear fruit.
And the Spirit of the Lord shall rest upon him.
The Spirit of wisdom and understanding, the Spirit of
counsel and might, the Spirit of knowledge and the
fear of the Lord. And his delight shall be in the fear of
the Lord." ~ Isaiah 11:1-3

Lynne's story

*My name is Lynne, I'm 32 years old, and this is my
story:*

*I live in a country where there is a powerful cultural
influence. I am married to a wonderful man who fills
me with happiness. I have everything a woman could
dream of with him. Unfortunately, we have no
children because my husband is sterile. I specify that
before our marriage, I already knew that he could not*

have children. However, that didn't stop me from marrying him. I love him so much, and my love for him is not limited to whether we have children. I would indeed have liked to have children, but if this is not the case, it is not a problem.

I give glory to God because everything God does is good. The Lord has given me a wonderful husband; I can only rejoice in this blessing. My husband is the eldest in his family, and during a family dinner, his parents made us understand that I had to have a child with my husband at all costs. However, knowing that the latter was infertile, his parents had found a solution to the problem.

Great was our surprise when they told us about their solution. Indeed, my in-laws informed us that my husband's little brother could have intimate relations with me to give offspring to my husband. I remain shocked by this indecent proposal to this day. My mother-in-law strongly influences her children, and any rebellion against her is almost impossible. She is against the decision we made to adopt a child. She specified that the only way to ensure this child had the same blood as my husband was to have a child with his brother.

My brother-in-law has been living with us ever since. My husband didn't say anything, but the atmosphere is agitated at home because my mother-in-law calls us daily for news. I let my husband know that it was out *of the question. He says he shares my views but doesn't know how to talk to his mother because she is becoming more stubborn. I don't want to lose my husband. In our culture, if I disobey my in-laws, they can find another wife for their son, my husband, without his consent.*

I decided to talk to my mother-in-law to bring her to her senses. I don't know how to approach the problem with her. This discussion with her will determine the future of my home. I'm so afraid she'll take it badly. I need the Lord to help me find the right words, to fill me with His wisdom, because I don't want to lose my husband. I am so desperate.

LYNNE.

The word of God teaches us that if Jesus Christ is in us, it is no longer we who live but He who lives in us. This word is a reality that every Christian must receive and bring to life within him. We no longer exist because there is someone else who controls our life. Our old nature (the old trunk) is dead. Instead, we have a new nature (a branch) with a new force. This new force is anchored in our new foundation, the substructure (its roots) on which our new nature lies. It is through him that the Lord directs our new nature. The Holy Spirit is the foundation of our new identity in Christ. He is proof that the Lord dwells in us. Only through Him can we make our relationship with God pleasant.

The Holy Spirit is nothing but the Spirit of God. As born-again Christians, that is, who have accepted Jesus Christ as our personal Savior and Lord, we do not have two spirits but one Spirit. In us, there is not our spirit and the Spirit of the Lord because our spirit dies and loses control of our life as soon as we receive Jesus Christ as Savior and Lord. This is why the Bible says that one cannot have two masters simultaneously because human desires and those of God are opposite.

It's a little hard to understand, but before our new birth in Christ, our life was under the control of an unclean spirit because we were unclean without God. This old, imperfect nature gave way to the Holy Spirit, the Spirit of God, and perfection and purity. This is why Galatians 2:19-20 tells us this: *through the law, I died to the law, that I might live for God. I have been crucified with Christ; yet I live, no longer I, but Christ lives in me; insofar as I live by faith in the Son of God who has loved me and given himself up for me.* Thus, our life is now under the dominion of our Lord Jesus Christ. He is our only Master.

Our nature died on the cross with all our carnal desires and passions. It can no longer dominate us. We have become perfect beings led by the Spirit of God through faith in Christ. We are perfect not because we do good but because we believe in a perfect God. If the Spirit of our God is continually in the person of Christ Jesus and

Christ dwells in us, then the Spirit of the Lord must constantly guide us and fully control our lives. The Word of God says, "But after faith has come, we are no longer under a tutor" (Galatians 3:25). It is this Spirit that gives us wisdom and discernment.

The Bible declares that the fear of the Lord is the beginning of wisdom. The Lord Jesus was full of wisdom because He feared God, and all His knowledge and power came from Him. He said: "By myself, I can do nothing; I judge only as I hear, and my judgment is just, for I seek not to please myself but him who sent me" (John 5:30). It is the same God who, through His Holy Spirit, filled King Solomon with wisdom. The Holy Spirit gave Him the discernment to solve the problems He faced in managing His kingdom. King Solomon's wisdom did not come to him from the many books he had read. It came straight to him from the Spirit of wisdom: the Holy Spirit.

In 1 Kings 3:16-28, the Bible presents the story of the two prostitutes who came to present themselves one day before King Solomon. Solomon meted out justice wisely in this story because the Spirit of God was with him. He didn't need the jury members to help him decide or to help him do justice. The Spirit of God alone was enough for him because our God is a God of justice, full of wisdom and discernment, who never clears the guilty. He knows everything, and He sees everything. He probes the hearts and minds. Nothing is hidden from His eyes.

Let's see the conclusion of this story in verse 28: *For they understood that God Himself had filled him with wisdom to do justice.* (1 Kings 3:28)

The Israelites knew that only God could fill a man with such wisdom. The Spirit of God in us is wiser than all human wisdom. The wisdom of God is foolishness to men. This Spirit reveals hidden things to us; He teaches us to honor the Lord by letting us know His will. Just because we pray, fast, or attend church does not mean we are called children of God. The Holy Spirit makes us Christians through our faith in Jesus Christ.

The Word made flesh penetrates us in the form of the Holy Spirit, and it is from this moment that we are called children of God. The Holy Spirit never takes pleasure in doing evil because He is a Spirit of righteousness and holiness. He delights in doing God's will in us. He cannot dwell in the lives of those who sin because He is holy. Therefore, we must trust Him by depending entirely on Him. We should not try to give Him directions or reason with Him because He is our God-sent guide. It is He who gives an account of our life to God.

The inexpressible prayer, the prayer with a sigh, the one that we make even when words are no longer enough to express ourselves before the Lord. It is also called "praying in tongues." The Holy Spirit makes all these prayers to God. It is He who speaks through us.

We pray in tongues and cannot translate this prayer. The Holy Spirit is the only one with the translation of the message released by our lips. God understands this spiritual language because no language has a secret for Him.

It is time to turn seriously to the Spirit of God and finally leave Him the role that the Lord has assigned to Him in us. The Lord listens to us through the Holy Spirit. So let him direct our lives according to his good pleasure. With him, we have the assurance that we are always in perfect communion with God.

The Bible says in Romans 14:17 that *the Kingdom of God is not a matter of what we eat or what we drink, but of living a life of goodness, peace, and joy in the Holy Spirit.* So, justice, love, peace, joy, and even wisdom must come from the Holy Spirit. This is why Jesus said that the peace He gives is different from the peace of this world. The peace of the Lord surpasses all understanding: it is a spiritual and eternal peace. It is the same with everything the Lord gives us. He tells us: *Be always joyful* because He knows that His Spirit within us can keep us satisfied, regardless of the times and circumstances.

We must understand that everything that comes to us from the Holy Spirit is of the order of the Spirit. Joy, love, peace, patience, kindness, faithfulness, gentleness, and self-control are no longer feelings but rather the mark of our spiritual character in Christ.

13

This is why in Galatians 5:22, the Bible speaks not of fruits but of the fruit of the Spirit. Thus, in Jesus Christ, all these character traits become one and no longer depend on us but on God. So, in Jesus, we can do everything because His Spirit enables us to do everything. We have to believe it, and we will see how wonderful it is to have God directing our whole life.

Today, if we could recommend a prayer to you, it would be this: "Holy Spirit, flood my heart with Your presence, in the mighty name of the Lord Jesus Christ."

My dear Lynne,

When you stand before your mother-in-law, "do not worry about knowing in advance what you will have to say but say the words which will be given to you at that time for they will not come from you but from the Holy Spirit" (Mark 13:11). "The Lord is with you, be strong, do not be discouraged. Your work will be rewarded" (2 Chronicles 15:7).

May the Lord Jesus fill you with wisdom through His Holy Spirit.

3

To be Active

"Whoever is slothful will not roast his game, but the
diligent man will get precious wealth."
~Proverbs 12:27

Letter from Albert

*My story is not a serious problem to some. However,
it is for me, and I must do something about it because
I can no longer pursue this path.*

Here is my story:

*I am a doctor; I love my job very much and thank God
I have nothing to complain about. I earn a perfect
living, and my little family lacks nothing. My problem
is that, for some time now, I no longer feel in my place.
I am convinced that I am called to do something else.
I no longer find great satisfaction in my profession. In
a word, I want to drop everything. I spoke about it
with my pastor, but he thinks I need rest, and it will*

pass. However, there is nothing. Everyone tells me I have a good life and asks me what else I want. I feel a void inside me that I want to fill. Therefore, I would like to take time for a spiritual retreat to know God's plan for my life.

My wife believes I'm worrying too much, that I better forget about it, and wonder what I would do If I had a job that paid much less than I have now. She may be right because I must confess that I am also afraid to know the truth. I have no peace. I want to know because I have more and more doubts. Therefore, I decided to pray and fast to know God's plan for my life. I'm tired of living with this doubt.
Did I make the right decision? Is it better that I continue with my current profession?

ALBERT.

This verse from the book of Proverbs shows the importance of working. The word of God encourages people to be active. Laziness is not good for a child of God because there are treasures to be reaped in activity for the Lord. Here, "activity" goes beyond our professional activity because we can work without harvesting the fruit or drawing satisfaction. Some people want to find a good job to feel productive; others want to create new things daily. They always need new challenges; otherwise, they feel unproductive. All these character traits are good and give meaning to our lives. However, we must always keep one thing in mind: In the word of God, it is said that "it is the blessing of the lord that makes rich, And He adds no sorrow to it (Proverbs 10:22). What is meant by "blessing of the Lord?"

The blessing of the Lord is a precious thing that God has provided for us, something that we will never be tired of, that will bring us complete satisfaction, and from which we will derive our wealth, an imperishable wealth. This blessing is found where God wants us to be active. The work the Lord wants us to do will bless us and many people. This activity, which is part of God's plan for our life, will never be followed by any sorrow. Even better, you will do it effortlessly and with love and joy. This activity is God's purpose for us and why God sent us to Earth.

The verse we read at the beginning of this chapter tells us that the diligent man will get precious wealth. This means that if our activity brings us no satisfaction or treasure except a salary at the end of the month, we must know that we are inactive for the Lord. There are attitudes we have and activities we do every day that bring no treasure to our lives. Actions that, after being taken, do not fill the void we feel. And yet, these things are very much a part of our lives. They are our daily life; we even think our life will have no meaning without them. However, when you think about it, these activities that we believe are vital only bring us partial well-being. We get no complete satisfaction from it. Our activity must satisfy us at all levels of our life. So then, when we are in God's perfect plan for our life, we are prosperous in every way. God provides for us in all areas of our lives because we do what He intended us to do on Earth. So, it is written in 3 John 1:2, *Beloved, I wish you to prosper in all things.*

The Lord does not give His blessing halfway. When He blesses us, we are blessed in every way. To be blessed by Him, we must not only be in the place God wants but also build our lives with things that are valuable to Him. God wants to bless us to be a blessing to other people. Know that if we are not in the right field of activity, many people are deprived of blessings because of us. Let's stop being active in the wrong domain and ask the Lord to make us functional in His plan. Let us pray that He will show us His plan for our life: In what area does He want us to practice? What is the purpose of our life? Why did God send us to Earth?

These questions need answers, and only the Lord can answer them because He wants us to be active in the right place. We are the only ones who are empowered to do this job. So, let's stop doing someone else's work; let everyone do their work and receive their blessings. Don't say that you have nothing to complain about in your job, that everything is fine, or that you think you are blessed, unlike many people. No, it's not for you to have reasoning that confirms you in your current position, although it seems more comfortable than most people around you, to be where God wants you to be. Let us understand that the blessing is not limited to material possessions because one can live in abundance and not be blessed. We all know at least one celebrity with everything the world could offer in comfort but still committed suicide. Let us ensure that our blessing truly comes from God because if God has not blessed, he who thinks he is blessed is not blessed.

Someone said, "If God has not blessed you, then the one who blessed you has cursed you." The Bible confirms this when it says that *Unless the Lord builds the house, those who build it labor in vain* (Psalm 127:1). When we are not in the right place chosen by God, all our efforts elsewhere are in vain. *"It is in vain that you get up early, go to bed late and struggle to earn your bread. The Lord gives so much to His beloved while they sleep"* (Psalm 127:2).

We waste much time and effort doing things not in God's plan. However, if we are in the right field, we will have less effort to make and more time to rest. Everyone has a specific activity chosen by our Creator. This is not just a job but something we have to do. From this activity, great blessings will flow straight from our Lord. An activity that we will do without effort, without compromising ourselves or complaining, and without seeking to be rich first. These are the characteristics of a high-value activity.

It must be understood that the Lord is the only one who

can reveal this activity to us: He is our Creator, and through Him, we can do everything. It's not about looking for what we do naturally. We are not talking about a gift of nature but a gift from the Lord, our God, and Creator. Doing something naturally does not necessarily mean that one was born for it. Some people know how to do several things and who do them well. It is not a guessing game; we should know our destiny. According to the Word of God, anything that does not result from a conviction is a sin. Conviction does not come from the ability to do or not do something. Our conviction must be based on what our God wants. It is from Him that our conviction must come.

The Lord Jesus was convinced of His mission on earth. Therefore, He exercised His ministry with joy and love, and contrary to what one might think, our Lord lacked nothing. He was special. He was doing things that people had never seen before, He spoke to the people in a different way than the doctors of the law, and until His death on the cross, he never had a shadow of doubt regarding his ministry. Jesus Christ is the best example to follow regarding effective activity. He has, through His actions, changed thousands of lives. Many have been, are, and will continue to be blessed through His work. When asked how He could do such amazing things, He didn't brag and say, "You know, I was born to do this." Instead, He responded by saying that He was only doing the work that His Father in Heaven had sent Him to do, which continues to bear fruit today. You and I are proof of that.

We must know the work the Lord has sent us to do on earth. We must realize it and fulfill it. If you have yet to know why you are on earth, ask the Lord to show you the work you are meant to do, the activity that He wants you to have, and from which you will obtain a blessing in all aspects. It is time for you to be at work, in an activity like your Father in Heaven. Jesus said: *My Father is always working and so am I* (John 5:17). Let us waste no more time on things our Lord did not plan for us. Let us be really at work where He wants us to be active.

Dear Albert,

To begin with, I would like you to know that anything that takes away peace from others should always be taken seriously.

Regarding your concern, you are on the right track. It is better to seek to know God's plan for you, especially when you have doubts. Only the One who sent you on earth knows your life's purpose. Isn't He the One who said He *knows the plans He has for you, plans to prosper you and not to harm you, plans to give you hope and a future (Jeremiah 29:11)?* It is, in fact, by seeking God's will for your life that *"you will know the truth, and the truth will set you free" (John 8:32).* However, when you know His perfect plan for you, remember that *"better is a little with the fear of the Lord than great treasure and trouble with it. (Proverbs 15:16)*

The blessing of the Lord is the only true wealth a man can possess because it never fails and is followed by no sorrow.

May the Lord our God reveal to you the work for which He has sent you on earth.

4

The Heart

"Above all else, guard your heart, for everything
you do flows from it."

~ Proverbs 4:23

Man looks at what strikes the eye, and that's normal
because it shines and draws attention. Nevertheless,
God looks at the heart because the heart never
pretends. It is as you are. It is your greatest treasure.
That is why you must take care of it by always keeping
it pure. Your heart's best friend is not you. It's not
even God. Your thoughts are the faithful friend of
your heart or instead, the best friend of your heart.
The heart and the thoughts form an inseparable
couple.

Man's eyes are on appearances, but those of the Lord
are on your heart and thoughts. Only God has access

to your thoughts. This is why you must always keep your heart and mind pure, for that is what strikes the eyes of God. The Bible says in Matthew 6:21, "For where your treasure is, there Your *heart will be also.*" This word also applies to God. Your heart is His treasure.

A touching testimony

> **The Abandoned Wife**

It is the story of a Christian woman going through challenging times in her home. Her husband had left her for another woman. He spent more time with her, gave her all kinds of gifts, romantic weekends, and nights in hotels, and wrote her the most beautiful love poems you can imagine. He said he only lived for the latter because they had things in common. The first thing he did when he got up in the morning was to text his mistress to find out how she had slept. Everything he had ever done for his wife; he was doing for her. He was ready to do the impossible, even if it meant humiliating his wife.

One day his wife, overwhelmed with pain, asked him to give her even one percent of the love he gave to his mistress, so great was her despair. Her husband no longer gave her any attention. At the slightest argument, this man threatened his wife with divorce. Despite the challenging context, the woman continued praying to God for her home, even though her husband no longer cared for her. Sometimes, when overwhelmed by the situation and her heart filled with anger, she would threaten her husband's mistress. Unfortunately, when her husband found out, he got furious and forced her to apologize to his mistress. But The Christian Woman always refused to do so; the angry husband began to beat her.

This couple's situation was going from bad to worse. Then, one day, the worst happened. After one of their many arguments, the Christian woman entered the marital bedroom and decided to kill herself despite her faith in God. She was in so much pain; she shed tears asking the Lord why she was suffering so much, asking Him how one could have Jesus Christ as Savior and have this kind of problem in life. She had wholly given her life to the Lord.

How could a Christian couple come to this? The wife had not been so lucky in life. She owed her life to the Lord, who had saved her from sickness, barrenness, ignorance, and death. She felt that the Lord was very far from her in this situation. Yet at no time in her life had she denied God. However, her pain at that moment was beyond anything she could imagine or think. She had suffered the worst physical and moral blows in her life. Yet, despite everything, she had always remained strong. She spent her nights crying, and her cheeks were constantly covered with tears. In her dismay, there was no one to console her. She felt like the Comforter who could revive her courage and strength was far from her.

No matter how much we cry out to the Lord, saying, "O Lord, do you not see my humiliation? Look how I am abandoned to my fate in a foreign land to make things worse. What have I done to deserve such contempt? Is there a pain comparable to mine?" The burden was too heavy to bear; it weighed down to the depths of her soul. She was suffering pierced through this woman's entire being. Her strength had left her, and even though the Holy Spirit in her was telling her to hold on, she couldn't because, at that very moment, the voice of the Spirit no longer echoed in her.

On this blow, the enemy had been the strongest. She felt like trash in the eyes of the man she loved. She was in distress, her whole inner being was in pain, and *her heart was overturning within her... Her house resembled that of death. We heard sighs but no one consoled her (Lamentation 1, verses 20-21).* Was she tested beyond her strength? No one could tell. Only the Lord could. He alone searches the heart and examines the mind. He alone knows the depths of our life. He has the answer to all our questions, and the word of the Lord teaches us that God does not test us beyond our strength.

When the test comes, He only acts when we feel we can't stand it any longer. The Bible teaches us that when we are weak, we are strong. Where does this strength come from? It comes to us from the Lord. The Lord is our strength; He is the rock we can lean on when we feel abandoned and hopeless. Generally, when we are distressed, these words of encouragement seem more theoretical than practical. We often ask ourselves whether God sees our misfortune, and why does He remain silent if He does see it?

This silence frequently leads us to distress. At this point, some, even the most devout Christians, come to think about suicide, even though the Bible fervently condemns this act. Our soul convinces us that this is the only option left to us when we have lost all hope: A lie never to be believed because, with God, there is always hope. Suicide should never be an option, whether we are Christians or not.

On Tuesday, March 5, 2013, at 4:20 pm in Seoul City, South Korea, this distressed wife left her infant child in the living room. He was watching television peacefully. Then, she entered her bedroom, thinking of ending her life.

➢ *The Prophet*

One day, a great prophet of God decided to make a five-day spiritual retreat to recharge his batteries with the Lord Jesus Christ. He managed to cut himself off from the world by staying in a room in his house and taking only one glass of water a day. In addition, he turned off his cell phone and told his wife and children not to disturb him during this time, no matter what. Our man of God, therefore, entered his room of refuge and began to pray, to meditate on the word of God.

On the first day, everything went very well. He received new directions from the Lord regarding his ministry. He carefully noted all these revelations he had received. On the night of the second day, while he was praying, the Holy Spirit revealed that the Lord wanted him to speak to someone on his behalf. God had a special message for this person, and He wanted the prophet to communicate that message. Being used to this type of revelation, the prophet said that as soon as he finished his retreat, he would try to know more about this message to communicate it to the person. He was in great demand as a prophet all over the world. People called from everywhere to consult him. That's one of the reasons he turned off his cell phone; he didn't want to be disturbed.

On the morning of the third day, as he was resting after a whole night of prayer, he heard the voice of the Lord asking him to call a person in danger. This person needed help. Through the prophet, the Almighty God wanted to tell this person that He had not abandoned him. However, the man of God put it off again, not understanding the urgency. He promised himself to do so as soon as he finished his retreat. "It's even the first thing I'll do," he thought.

Throughout the day, God's call became increasingly insistent, so the prophet could no longer concentrate on his prayer time. Finally, he felt like a weight in his heart on the night of the third to the fourth day. This weight was so heavy and painful that he asked God about the nature of this pain. So, he replied that it is a pain of a soul in distress crying out to Him.

- Lord, if it is Your will that I now speak to this person, let Your will be done. Allow that person to call me now to talk to him on your behalf.

After saying this prayer, the prophet opened his phone, which had been turned off since the beginning of his retreat. He began to pray that God would allow this person to contact him. As he prayed, the Spirit of God revealed to him that it was not the person who should call him but instead, he who should do it. So, without overthinking, he picked up his phone and, guided by the Holy Spirit, began dialing a phone number. It was Tuesday, March 5, 2013, at 3:20 am in New York in the United States. *"Out of my distress I called on the Lord, and He answered me, setting me free...the Lord is for me; He comes to my help" (Psalms 118:5-7).*

> ### The call to salvation

The phone rang several times, but the woman wouldn't answer.

- I want to be left alone. Is that too much to ask? she thought, crying. But the phone kept ringing.

- Lord, I hope it is not too late; please allow this person to pick up his phone, said the prophet praying. When she looked at her cell phone, the young lady realized it was an international call. However, she didn't seem to know that number. It was the area code for the United States. She decided to take the call, even though she wasn't feeling well.

- Hello?

- Yes, hello, hello.

- Hello. Whom am I speaking to, please?

- Sorry for calling you at such a late hour of the night. I'm calling you from New York. It's 3 am here. I am curious to know what time it is where you are or even what country you are in.

- It does not matter, sir; you do not disturb me. It is 4 pm here, and I am in South Korea, precisely in Seoul.

- Thank you, Madam. I am a prophet of God, and for three days, I cut myself off from the world and my family for a prayer retreat. During these times of meditation, God put it on my heart to call you because he had an important message for you. Your phone number was communicated to me by the Holy Spirit.

On the other end of the line, the woman started crying. This time it was tears of joy, the joy of knowing that the God of the universe had not forgotten her, that He cared about her, He the Almighty, the Creator of Heaven and Earth! What more could she want? She wanted to look only at this God who can do everything and to whom nothing is impossible. He had heard her cry and come to her rescue by touching a stranger so that she would know He loved her, and she was important to Him.

The prophet and the woman had a long conversation. He gave her the message that God had for her. The woman asked him all the questions that haunted her. He responded by dispelling all his fears. As they spoke, the woman's whole being was filled with peace that surpassed all understanding. The prophet was only an instrument. This woman was in conversation with God. It was Him talking to her.

Men can look down on you, humiliate you, abandon you, and hurt you in different ways. If God is for you, then fear not. Never take revenge. Forgive and move on. There is only one person who gave His life for you. If he did, it's because he knows your value, and you are valuable to him. A person who did not give his life for you cannot understand your true value.

After her conversation with the man of God, this woman's outlook completely changed. Now that she knew the God of the universe was watching over her and was in control of her life, she no longer dwelled on what she could experience in her home. She had surrendered everything in the hands of God. She needed peace, and God had given her His peace. She dried her tears and raised her head with hope for a better tomorrow. The Lord told her that 2013 was her last year of suffering and mourning. Before the end of this year, He was going to open a new door in her life. This woman's joy was at its height because God's clock for her destiny was ticking. God always gives us more than we can imagine or think. Whatever your condition, know that you are precious in His eyes. You must consider what He tells you, not what people say or think about you. If God says you are a wonderful creature, then you must believe it, no matter how the mirror reflects you or even the mocking gaze of people. Your value is not physical but spiritual, like your God. He looks at your heart, not your physique.

The feelings of rejection, contempt, indifference, abandonment, and others are only the fruit of our trust in human beings. We place our trust in people of the exact nature as us. We feel humiliated, betrayed, or cheated when these people disappoint us. These feelings are only the consequence of our dependence on others. If the world exists, there will always be disappointments; there will always be people who will not keep their promises, will despise you, and will put you through hell. There will always be people who, after hurting you, will never ask you for forgiveness or pay attention to you. This type of person will always exist and will not change tomorrow. If you trust a man completely, expect to be disappointed. It won't happen every day, but it can happen. Even the Word of God has warned us about this. Indeed, here is what the Lord says on this subject: Cursed *is the one who trusts in man, who draws strength from mere flesh, and whose heart turns away from the Lord* (Jeremiah 17:5). The Lord alone is faithful and sure support; therefore, it is *better to trust in the Lord than to put confidence in man* (Psalms 118:8).

The real problem is not others but us. No one in this world will be judged by what others did to them. We will stand in judgment before God for our actions. No one will justify himself before God by saying, "Lord, I acted this way because this person first did such or such thing to me." We will be judged for our sins. It doesn't matter what people do to you in the sight of God. It is your actions that matter. It is important to understand this well because we can never say it enough: salvation is personal. Each of us will carry our burden. The word of God is very clear: *God is not mocked, for whatever one sows, that will he also reap* (Galatians 6:7). Even if it is not easy, let us strive to sow acts that please God, and this is only possible if we allow the Holy Spirit to lead our lives. What will be the use of obeying our flesh if it means spending all our eternity in hell?

In the testimony above, we see how God intervened in the life of this woman who was despised and abandoned by her husband. She was ready to kill herself; she thought God had forgotten her and was insensitive to her ordeal. She was far from imagining that the Lord had His eyes on her from the height of His throne of glory. As she was precious in His eyes,

He did not allow her to end her life. Instead, he restored and strengthened her so she could do what He had sent her on Earth to do. Misfortune was not part of the plans He had for her. She still had a future, and this future, contrary to what she thought, was full of hope.

People don't have to do us good or like us. However, by the love of God, we are called to love our neighbor as ourselves and to overcome the evil that others do to us with good. What should matter most to us is to do the will of our Father in heaven. Even in distress when all seems lost, and we have no way out. Do not deny God by having a behavior that does not honor Him because it will only aggravate your situation. Instead, you need to entrust the problem you are facing to Him. God always has a solution because He is the solution you need. If you open your Bible, you will see that others before you have faced these trials, sometimes worse than yours. These people cried out to the Lord, and the Lord answered them. So, tell yourself that what He has done for others, He will certainly do it for you. I don't know your problem or the trial you are facing. The only thing I know and what I am convinced of is that your situation is no worse than Job's. The story of Job that the Bible relates is that of an irreproachable man, faithful to God and fulfilled by life.

This man was deprived of everything: his children

(who all died the same day), health, and property. *Yet, despite everything, Job did not sin or accuse God of doing wrong* (Job 1:22). On the contrary, he continued to give thanks to God. See what he replies when his wife asks him to curse God and die: *If we accept happiness from God, why should we refuse misfortune from him?* Whether it is happiness or misfortune, everything God does is good. The Lord is a refuge for all who rely on Him in times of trouble. He does not abandon those who turn to Him.

If, like the woman in the testimony, you are downhearted and hopeless, let the Lord know your sorrow in these words:

Lord,

"I pray to you, my protector.
You will send help from heaven and save me,

But you will bring trouble on my attackers.
You are faithful, and you can be trusted."
(Psalm 57:2-3)

Because *"Only God gives inward peace, and I depend on him.*
God alone is the mighty rock that keeps me safe, and He is the fortress where I feel secure.

God saves me and honors me.
He is that mighty rock where I find safety.
Trust God, my friends, and always tell him each of
your concerns.
God is our place of safety." (Psalm 62:6-8)

I will always trust You, for Your goodness is worth
more than life.

In Jesus Name, I have prayed.

5

The Covenant of Marriage

"Therefore, a man leaves his father and his mother
and cleaves to his wife, and they become one flesh."
~ Genesis 2:24

Gustave's letter

*I am facing a dilemma; I am married and a father of
2 children. My problem is the following: I no longer
love the mother of my children; I no longer feel
anything for her because I am in love with another
woman. I don't know how it happened, but I love
another woman who makes me happy, and she, too, is
madly in love with me. With the latter, I feel good.*

*I feel things that I have never felt for my wife. Yet my
wife and I got married very young. It will soon be nine
years since we have been married.*

With my mistress, it's crazy love. We can no longer do

without each other. I don't have that same bond with my wife. I even happened to be violent with her. I no longer desire my wife, whereas with the other woman, it's different. Everything about her makes me happy; I feel like I've found my soul mate. I know adultery is a sin, and I no longer know where I am. My wife would like us to have other children, but I don't want to because I want to divorce her so badly to be with the love of my life.

I am ready to abandon my wife and start a new life with her, and it is with her that I would like to have other children. What should I do? My children are still very young. It is for them that I still hesitate to divorce. However, on the other hand, I don't know if I can bear living away from my mistress any longer. I need the Lord to help me because I can't stand this situation anymore.

GUSTAVE.

When I had just become born again, I thought life in Christ was life in pink, if I may say so. I believed anyone married in the church was safe from divorce, adultery, and domestic violence. Knowing some realities that Christian couples live, I realize that we sometimes live the same realities as those who are not Christians. It's hard to say, but it's the truth. We are all made of flesh,

41

and when we don't watch over our spiritual life as children of God, our flesh eventually wins out and turns us away from the presence of God. The word of God tells us, *"Watch and pray so that you will not fall into temptation; the Spirit is willing, but the flesh is weak."* (Matthew 26:41)

Anyone who considers himself a Christian and does not let the Holy Spirit lead his life will have difficulty resisting temptation. He whom the Holy Spirit does not lead is guided by his nature, the flesh. *Now the works of the flesh are evident: sexual immorality, impurity, sensuality, idolatry, sorcery, enmity, strife, jealousy, fits of anger, rivalries, dissensions, divisions, envy, drunkenness, overeating, and things like these* (Galatians 5:19-21). Those who do such things will not inherit the kingdom of God.

Gustave's case is not unique to men. Some women also commit adultery. The family unit is the object of several evils mentioned in the biblical verse above, regardless of whether one is a Christian or not. All social categories are affected by this reality. Marriage is the commitment to love an imperfect person unconditionally for the rest of our lives. It is not a contract but a covenant. This covenant is not something to be taken lightly: it is a commitment that must be respected. When we make a promise to someone, we must keep that promise. God wants us to be people of word who do not violate their commitments. "When you make a vow to God, do not

42

delay fulfilling it; for he has no pleasure in fools. Pay what you have vowed." (Ecclesiastes 5:4)

As a child of God, when you have committed, you must keep it. Indeed, sometimes it's not easy because people can change, especially in the context of marriage. We sometimes face other realities regarding the person we are in covenant with. Things may not go the way we want; it can happen. However, this does not justify breaking this alliance. Whether the person is good or bad, it doesn't matter. The engagement can be broken, but not the marriage. Engagement is a covenant promise, while marriage is a lifelong covenant. By marrying, we become one being. *Thus, they are no longer two but one flesh* (Matthew 19:6). However, we live in an imperfect world filled with wickedness, human weaknesses, and hard-heartedness.

In such an environment, anything can happen, especially when we conform to the world. It may happen that, as in the case of Gustave, a person commits adultery. Even then, the Bible recommends forgiveness because divorce, as Jesus Christ said, is a sign of the harshness of a man's heart. I am speaking here to people of faith; we must not act as in the world. Reconciliation and forgiveness must be part of the life of a child of God. It's a shame to see that the divorce rate in the church is growing as much as in the world. It was not so in the beginning. Do you think Adam wanted to divorce Eve after the Lord rebuked him for eating the fruit of the knowledge of good and evil? He was angry, but he stayed with Eve, his wife. He was one flesh with her.

Today, some people marry and say, "If it doesn't work out, I can always divorce and marry another man or woman." Would they have had the same thought on a desert island? I do not think so. They would not have thought this way if they were alone with their spouse on earth. They would have made things better. The Bible only condones divorce when adultery is involved; even then, we can forgive. Yet many Christians have divorced for reasons that sometimes have nothing to do with infidelity. People divorce for misunderstandings and behavioral issues or any reason. The list is long, and cheating is not included. As children of God, we must seek solutions to our problems with the Lord. Let us take an example from the Father through His word. If I am imperfect, I cannot claim perfection from my husband. Only God is perfect.

Marriage is a commitment between two imperfect people that requires unconditional love. Let's tolerate each other and not try to justify ourselves when things go wrong. In a couple, each part is responsible for the other as they form one entity. Let us manifest love as the book of Corinthians teaches us: *"love is patient and kind; love does not envy or boast; it is not arrogant and rude. Love bears all things, believes all things, hopes all things, and endures all things"* (1 Corinthians 13:4-8). When we get married, we swear fidelity in love and mutual respect. If one of the spouses uses verbal or physical violence, there is infidelity to the marriage oath. However, we must also understand that adultery is not the greatest sin in marriage. Besides, there are no big or small sins.

God hates all forms of sin. Whether it is a man who cheats on his wife or a wife who does not respect her husband, both are an abomination before God. Just because someone is in alliance with us doesn't mean they must tolerate our bad behavior. We must make the life of our neighbor pleasant under the covenant; it is our responsibility. The marital home should be a haven of peace, not a place of argument, fear, or terror. Let us not be a cause of stumbling for the other person; by doing so, we make ourselves guilty in the eyes of God. We must do everything to ensure that the covenant is respected. Everyone must do their part and not mutually blame each other or think they have already done their part because it is a matter of communion. According to God, marriage is a source of life that draws its power from Jesus Christ, the primary source of life, and gives life to our source. Whatever sin we have committed, if we sincerely ask the Lord for forgiveness and do not do it again, He will forgive us.

According to the law of Moses, the adulterous woman in the Bible was to be stoned to death. Jesus knew the law and the sentence that must be applied. The Doctor of Law also knew the law of Moses. Even the adulterous woman knew the fate reserved for her. Yet, when asked the question, Jesus responded by saying, "Let *any one of you who is without sin be the first to throw the stone at her.* (John 8:7)

What had the doctors of the law done after hearing Jesus' answer? *"They went away one at a time"* (John 8:9). They did not admit that any of them were without sin. The Lord does not encourage adultery; the Bible is clear on that. We must not commit adultery. But, if someone sins and repents, the Lord will no longer hold it against him because God is love. Let us, therefore, not condemn our neighbor when God himself does not condemn him. Let's read the end of the story: "Neither *do I condemn you, says Jesus. Go and from now on, sin no more."* (John 8:11)

See how the Lord solves this problem. First, he showed His mercy to this adulteress. He did not condemn her. He is aware that this woman knows she has done wrong. Therefore, He asked her not to do it again. Otherwise, she would be condemned. And that's what usually happens in some divorce cases; People ask for forgiveness but resume their same habits as if nothing had happened. This means that their repentance is not sincere. And in this case, there is betrayal and non-respect of the covenant.

A covenant is only made between two people within the framework of marriage, as with the Lord, for that matter. We cannot bring other partners into our covenant with our spouse and want our home to be a haven of peace. It's like setting our house on fire and being the first to shout fire. It is because of the harshness of our hearts, as the Lord said that there is divorce. Many people are tormented in their households by their husbands. Some people have contracted HIV because of their spouse's infidelity; others are paralyzed for life because of domestic violence. Many people are murdered by their spouses, and Christians are not spared. Some even go so far as to have sex with their lover or mistress in the marital bed, even though they know that the Lord recommends that *"Marriage should be honored by all, and the marriage bed kept pure"* (Hebrews 13: 4). When you dishonor yourself and your marriage even though you know what God's word says about it, how do you expect your partner to react?

You are one flesh with your spouse, so whatever harm you do to that person, you do it to yourself. And if this person forgives you despite that, do not do it again. So, likewise, do not abuse your neighbor; if you have the chance to restore your marriage, do it so that this time it can last all your life as the Lord intended. Indeed, when God created the first couple, Adam and Eve, the marriage covenant was meant to last for life, regardless of the trials that may arise. We cannot separate what God has sealed. *"Therefore, what God has joined together, let no one separate"* (Matthew 19:6). Unfortunately, many of us are forced to break this covenant at the risk of losing our lives. We might even wonder if God really joined them because everything that God joins together should last, and no sorrow is added to it. The truth is that not every marriage that happens is God's will. This may shock you, but it is a sad reality.

⁓❧⁓

Let's take an example:

You are a single woman in a relationship with a married man. You consider yourself a Christian. The man you are in a relationship with tells you that he is not happy with his wife and that it is with you that he finds his happiness. This man no longer takes care of his family. It is with you that he travels, and he offers you the most beautiful gifts.

As for his wife, she is reduced to the role of housekeeper. When she complains about her husband's behavior, he starts beating her. She has become the object of all humiliation. This man ends up divorcing his wife and marries you. Your marriage was even blessed in church. I have a question: do you think God approves your marriage? A marriage that was engineered on someone else's misfortune. Beloved, it is not because we marry in a church that God approves this union. You don't build your happiness on someone else's misfortune.

We must seek God's will in our relationship before getting married. We must present the person we want to spend the rest of our days with to the hands of the

Lord through prayer so that He may guide us in our decision. We must not take the covenant of marriage lightly. We must build our union according to the principles of God because *"unless the Lord builds the house, those who build it labor in vain."* (Psalms 127:1)

In the Old Testament, we see that the repeated infidelities of the people of Israel never caused the Lord to abandon His faithfulness and covenant with His people. God remains faithful even when we are unfaithful. He never broke His covenant with us despite our sins; He never even regretted making a covenant with us. As it is written, *God does not take back his gifts, he does not change his mind about those he has chosen* (Romans 11:29). He honors and respects His covenant with us. So, let's follow His example by honoring our marriage commitments and obeying the Lord.

Before being in alliance with our husband or wife, we are first in covenant with God; this alliance is the base and foundation of the marriage alliance. It is He who sustains our marriage. If we defile our marriage, we are defiling the temple of God. When you commit to marriage, you must honor that commitment. As a Christian, not only have you committed to your spouse, but above all, you have committed to God and before God. The Lord sealed this covenant that He did not force you to make. The first place in your life belongs to God.

Our neighbor's bad behavior must not influence our relationship with God and separate us from the Lord. It is written in the book of Romans that *"nor height, nor depth, nor any other creature shall be able to separate us from the love of God, which is in Christ Jesus our Lord"* (Romans 8:39). Your wife or husband is that other creature that this verse is talking about. So also, this creature must not separate you from the love of God. Your covenant with God is above your marriage. Rely on your covenant with God to make your marriage happy. Don't try to change your life partner but pray that the Lord changes the person, transforms you, and always controls your marriage. Trust in Him, and everything will be fine because nothing is impossible with God.

Dear Gustave,

God isn't pleased with you because *"He knows you have been unfaithful to the wife you married when you were young. You promised that she would be your partner, but now you have broken that promise. Didn't God create you and your wife to become like one person? And why did He do this? It was so you would have children, and then lead them to become God's people. Don't ever be unfaithful to your wife. The Lord God All-Powerful of Israel hates anyone who is cruel enough to divorce his wife. So take care never to be unfaithful!" (Malachi 2:14-16)*

"You should be faithful to your wife,
Just as you take water from your own well.
And don't be like a stream from which just any woman may take a drink.
Save yourself for your wife and don't have sex with other women.
Be happy with the wife you married when you were young.
She is beautiful and graceful, just like a deer;
You should be attracted to her and stay deeply in love." (Proverbs 5:15-19)

"Be reconciled to the Lord, trust in Him, renounce sin and all will be well. You know, "There is a way that seems right to a man, but its end is the way to death.
(Proverbs 14:12)

May God have mercy on you and help you restore your home.

6

The Power of Silence

"The Lord will fight for you; you need only to be
still."
Exodus 14:14

Lucy's letter

*I am a 16-year-old teenager, motherless since the age
of 5. I live with my father and my stepmother. The
latter does not love me and does everything to
separate me from my father. I hardly live with them
because she enrolled me in a boarding school, and
even on weekends, I cannot come home. I only come
during the holidays, like right now. I tried to talk to
my father about it, but he didn't react. He loves this
woman so much that he does whatever she asks.*

*There are days when my father is away; my
stepmother refuses to let me sit in the living room,
yells at me for nothing, reduces my pocket money, and
sometimes even prevents me from going out. Yet, out*

of love for my father, I remained calm and never disrespected my stepmother. I put up with all this suffering because I tell myself that since I'm doing well in school, I'll be in college in a year and won't have to put up with it anymore. But since last night, I've been exhausted, and if things continue like this, I'll come to blows with her. Can you imagine I found her in my room reading my diary when I returned from church yesterday? I was so shocked that I told her she had no right and that it was my private life.

She replied that I had no private life in her house and that she had the right to do worse than read my diary. At the same time, she took the photo of my mother by my bedside, broke the frame, and tore the picture into a thousand pieces, adding that if I was sick of her, I just had to join my mother.

I was paralyzed; I wanted to fight with her. It happened yesterday and today. I'm writing to you because I know I won't be able to hold out for long. The next time this woman tries to harm me, even with a simple word, I will not let it go. I did everything I could to honor my parents as the word of God recommends. But unfortunately, this woman does not love me.

My strength is dwindling, I feel weak, and I know that I will not be able to control myself the next time she misbehaves because, besides God, I am the only one that can protect myself from this woman. Please give me a comforting word! What does the Bible advise in *such a situation?*

LUCY.

It is challenging to remain silent when faced with a situation that troubles us. When we face a trial, we tend to cry out our pain for some or confide in a friend for others. We are trying to get out of this situation. We think of everything except keeping calm. Children of God sometimes forget the Lord's promises when things go wrong. As soon as we have problems, we open our mouths, and without even consulting the Holy Spirit, we start talking and complaining instead of remaining silent.

Talking too much is a sin *because too much talk leads to sin* (Proverbs 10:19). This attitude reflects the state of our hearts. We are full inside and want to pour all our pain out. We want to understand why this is happening to us and not to someone else. Indeed, it is normal to feel bad and even more normal not to keep in us all that is eating away at us. Therefore, opening your heart and looking for someone you can confide in is good. The Lord Jesus even said, *"For the mouth speaks what the heart is full of"* (Matthew 12:34). It's good to empty your heart. However, it must be done by being led by the Spirit of God to avoid doing an act we will regret later. Let us always remember that one day we will give an account to God for all our actions as it is written in the Bible: "So then, every one of us should give an account of himself to God." *(Romans 14:12)*

In some situations, it is best to remain silent. It is not an attitude of weakness but a spiritual disposition. Whatever the test, it will never be beyond our strength. The Lord will always give us the strength and the ability to overcome this trial. When we face a problem, always take the example of the life of the Lord Jesus on earth. He was not a talkative person. He did not speak to please men but to meet a need. His words were always full of life. Even in the face of trial, He kept silent. Knowing how to stay quiet is an excellent mark of power. The book of Proverbs states, "Whoever is patient has a great understanding, but one who is quick-tempered displays folly" (Proverbs 14:29). There are too many useless words coming out of our mouths. We will win in any situation by staying calm. So, let's stop complaining, judging, or criticizing, even if we are right. Let us remain silent; our God will speak for us. He is our defender. Let us be silent if the Holy Spirit does not want us to speak. This will save us from sin. We must remain silent once we have committed our fate to the Lord. We cannot start talking when the Lord is fighting for us. Even if it is hard, we must be quiet because we have nothing to say when God is at work.

Let's look at the story of the Israelites when they captured the city of Jericho. This is the story of a prominent people with a powerful army and their priests who walked around the city of Jericho for six days without speaking, in total silence. *"Joshua had commanded the people themselves to be perfectly silent and not to shout the battle cry until they gave the order"* (Joshua 6:10). The people remained silent, and only the trumpets were heard.

This story shows that it is not shouting or a mighty army that gives victory but the deliverance hand of the Lord of hosts. He is the one who fights for us; he is the solution and the answer we need when everything goes wrong. If you have spoken to God in prayer or presented the situation troubling you, remain calm and do not get agitated. Only believe, keep the faith, and trust Him; you will see how He will work for you. The Bible tells you, *"Why are you in despair, o my soul? And why are you disturbed within me? Hope in God, for I shall again praise him, the help of my countenance and my God"* (Psalm 43:5). When you are in trouble, before talking to anyone, first submit your problem to the Lord. He will give you the directives or direct you to a mature person who will know how to advise you.

Your strength is not in the abundance of complaints or words but in the Lord, your strength. Put all your trust in Him and patiently wait for His response, even if He delays. As the Word of God says in Isaiah 30:15, "In quietness and trust is your strength." This verse alone sums up everything we have just said. Silence is an effective weapon against those who wish us harm.

Staying calm when things are going badly is a powerful strategy in a fight. Indeed, if we are allowed to speak, it is by prayer, by entrusting ourselves continually to God until He comes to our rescue and gives us victory over our opponents. Only God has the right to speak in our battles.

Don't say to yourself, "I can't stay calm; I must do something. I must defend myself. I have my say." Don't, beloved. If anyone has a say in it, it's God, not us. Therefore, before speaking, we must always ask ourselves if what we will say is worth more than our silence because silence can sometimes make us understand what words can't. We don't have to prove anything to anyone; we don't have to respond to attacks: it will only make things worse and risk angering us. But *"man's anger does not produce the righteousness that God desires."* (James 1:20)

Anger and revenge are simply the results of our lack of calm and tranquility. God's Word encourages us daily to *"be quick to hear, but slow to speak, and slow to anger"* (James 1:19). We can only put this word into practice if we make calm and tranquility our strength and by trusting entirely in the Lord. The Lord is our strength; He is the mighty warrior strong in our battles. Let us look to Him, and He will do us justice.

Dear Lucy,

I understand your dismay in this situation. However, you have already shown much patience. As you said yourself, you have only the Lord. So, keep silent before Him, wait patiently on Him. You see, my dear Lucy, sometimes silence is the best response to those who hurt us. So don't waver at your father's wife because "it is not by strength that one prevails" *(1 Samuel 2:9)*. *"He only is my rock and salvation: he is my defense; I shall not be moved. In God is my salvation and my glory; the rock of my strength, and my refuge is in God." (Psalm 62:6-7)*

Here is how you should pray to God in the face of this situation that is destabilizing you:

"You see everything, Lord! Please don't keep silent or stay so far away.

Fight to defend me, Lord God, and prove I am right by your standards.

Don't let "her" laugh at me or say to each other, "Now we've got what we want! We'll gobble her up."

Disappoint and confuse all who are glad to see me in trouble; disgrace and embarrass my proud enemies who say to me, "You are nothing." (Psalm 35:22-26)

It is in the name of Jesus Christ that I have prayed.

Amen

And there you have the Lord's answer to your prayer.

Lucy,

Above all, do not let yourself be intimidated by her.

"Get yourself ready! Stand up and say to them whatever I command you. Do not be terrified by them, or I will terrify you before them. Today I have made you a fortified city, an iron pillar, and a bronze wall to stand against the whole land... They will fight back but they won't win. I, the Lord, give my word. I won't let them harm you." (Jeremiah 1:17-19)

May the Lord protect and strengthen you.

7

The Shadow of Death

"Even though I walk through the valley of the
shadow of death, I will fear no evil, for you are with
me."
~ Psalm 23:4

Letter from Grace

*With a heavy heart, I am writing this letter to you; my
story is so sad. I ask you in advance to forgive me if
my words offend you. I need to get out of the night I'm
in. I must free myself by revealing this heavy burden
that has weighed on me for months. As far back as I
can remember, I have always dedicated my life to the
Lord.*

*At 15, I committed my life to Him and accepted Him
as my personal Savior and Lord. I do not doubt my
love and my faith in the Lord. I don't understand how
I got to such a level of debauchery. I cannot explain it.
Nobody knows. Nobody sees me. There are only four*

witnesses, four who know what I'm doing.
And believe me, that's enough to make me feel guilty.

1-God sees me and knows it.

2-I see me, and I know.

3-My computer, the tool of this debauchery, knows what I'm doing.

4-The father of debauchery and sin, the devil, sees me and tells me it does not matter.

It all started when my husband cheated on me with this other woman. He was no longer the same. He had changed entirely and no longer wanted to have sex with me. He no longer touched me and pushed me away each time I approached him. Sometimes he told me he was exhausted. I felt humiliated and suffered in silence about his behavior. I did everything to be attractive, but he only had eyes for his mistress. Even when he was home, he spent most of his time on his tablet talking with her and didn't care if I was there. He completely ignored me. To avoid arguments, I kept quiet because I was tired of complaining.

It wasn't easy to live. He organized trips and outings with her in which the main objective was to satisfy all their sexual desires. My husband's whole life revolved around this relationship. She sent him videos of her in case she was absent: at least he wouldn't miss it. When they weren't together, they were doing it on the net, no matter where, at work or home. When he went to bed late at night, he fell asleep because he had just made love. That is how the spirit of perversion entered my home. We sometimes went five or even seven to eight months without him touching me. It bothered me but not him. In bed, he avoided me altogether. The truth is that he was faithful to his mistress. He proudly told her he didn't touch me in bed and pushed me away when I tried to touch him. This is how it all started. I was young, and from the top of my 26 years, I was full of sexual desires.

Sometimes the desire consumed me, and I had to contain myself. The few times I had intimate relationships with my husband, he didn't get involved. One day, tired of this situation, I opened my computer and visited a porn site. I was disgusted with these things; I became a regular on these sites when I was alone at home or when my husband was moving. I was watching these videos while masturbating. Each time I asked the Lord for forgiveness by telling Him I would not do it again, this distanced me from Him and defiled me. Unfortunately, I had a hard time resisting. I no longer approached my husband because he no longer wanted me. I would go to a porn site when I needed to have intimate relationships. It lasted six months until I decided to stop everything and no longer succumb to temptation. I was ashamed of myself, and I knew that the Lord saw me and that it was marked in my book of life.

Nothing justified my depraved behavior. Nothing, not even my husband's lack of affection and infidelity. Even if he neglected me, that was no reason to indulge in debauchery. It was fornication in the sight of the Lord. I felt dirty and soiled. I am not proud of myself because it contradicts my values and the education I received. It's been two months since I quit, and I feel better. My husband has not changed his attitude toward me. However, it no longer hurts me because I have put this situation in the hands of the Lord. His will be done.

The problem I have right now, and that's why I'm writing to you, is that despite my prayers and fasting, I don't feel completely restored. It's as if the shadow of this sin is following me. I am very afraid to dive again. I feel like this shadow walks by my side every day. This worries me because I have the feeling that death is following me. I asked the Lord for forgiveness, I even confided in a friend, and we fasted and prayed together. Things are back to normal, but the fear of falling back remains. I want to overcome this shadow that I feel like death is by my side, which makes me believe that I am not entirely free from this hold. Is it normal to handle this kind of fear? Does that mean I'm going to dive back in? My salvation is the most precious thing in life. I need help.

GRACE.

In the Epistle to the Philippians, in chapter 3, verse 13 is written: *"I do one thing: I forget what is behind me and 'I' strive to achieve what is in front of me."* This passage describes the attitude we must adopt when we become new creatures in Christ.

Once we have made Jesus Christ our personal Savior and Lord, our past remains behind us. The Lord wipes out and forgets all our sins through the spiritual process of being born again. Our God is a God who does not cling to negative memories because He is Holy. Therefore, He focuses only on the best of us in His relationship with us. Through His word and under the action of the Holy Spirit, He teaches us how to be like Him because He is Holy, and His word declares that we were created in His image; our God wants us to be holy like Him. *"Be holy because I, the Lord your God, am holy."* (Leviticus 19:2)

We cannot become saints or lead a life that glorifies God if we feel condemned daily or constantly reminded of our past mistakes. God is love, and He means it when He tells us that our sins are forgiven. Here is what He says: *"He who conceals his transgressions will not prosper, but whoever confesses them and forsakes them obtains mercy"* (Proverbs 28:13). Divine mercy is that goodness of God by which He forgives our faults and renews us in our dignity, so that we can rise again, and that God's plan of love may be fulfilled in us. Therefore, God's forgiveness derives from this divine mercy which encourages indulgence towards a person who has committed a sin and repents from it. So, no one can condemn us when God has acquitted us. Nobody, not even ourselves, and it does not depend on our feelings or the seriousness of the fault. We must believe in His word and have faith that He has washed away our sins and cleansed us through the power of the blood of Jesus Christ. The devil will do everything in his power to make us think that we cannot be forgiven so quickly, he will make us believe that we are too weak to be able to resist him and that, sooner or later, we will end up falling back into sin. As for men, they will condemn and judge us and never trust us again. We may lose friends due to our faults.

Everything can happen, but it will not change the word of God and His love for us. Indeed, His word does not change and never will. What He said is written and engraved for eternity: It declares that *"if we confess our sins, He is faithful and just to forgive us, and to cleanse us from all unrighteousness"* (1 John 1:9). We must put our faith in this word and firmly believe that this is what happens when we sin and confess our sins to Him. He then forgives us, and He purifies us. Through his sacrifice on the cross, the Lord Jesus Christ washed away our sins. Why does He wash away our sins? Quite simply, on the one hand, so that no one comes to hold it against us, and on the other hand, because the Lord Himself no longer wants to remember our past faults.

The only way to forgive something is to forget it. The best way to forget is to have no longer what we want to forget in front of us or our thoughts. The Lord, our God, forgets all the transgressions we confess to Him, "all without exception" for eternity. So, if our Creator, the One who holds our life in His hands, completely forgets our transgressions, then there is no reason why we should not do the same.

It will do us no good to live in guilt or fear of a possible relapse into sin. The precious blood of Jesus Christ is the stronghold of protection that ensures that the devil can never hold us captive again. By His blood, we are forgiven of our sins and are now at peace with God. So, there is no more condemnation. The blood of our Lord has delivered us from our sins by cleansing our conscience from the works of death. We have been set free by faith in His word. You know, the devil's specialty is lies. He is the father of lies. In this world, no one trusts a liar. So why do we like to pay attention to the lies the devil injects into our thoughts? We must repel it with the authority of the name of Jesus Christ, the Way, the Truth, and the Life. We must heed His words, not those of the devil. The Bible says that God does not lie and never repents His blessings. He never regrets the good He does. Even when we are unfaithful, He remains faithful.

The word of God teaches us that when we are in Christ, *old things are passed away; behold, all things have become new* (2 Corinthians 5:17). Once confessed and forgiven, sin is no longer part of our present but remains in the past. As we know, the past is never ahead but always behind us. When we walk, we fix our eyes in front of us. No one can go backward. To step back is to go back, to return to the past. Why always look back when we know that the best is yet to come, so ahead and not behind us? Psalm 23 in verse 4 tells us this: *Even when I walk through the valley of the shadow of death, I fear no evil for You are with me.* I want to dwell on the expression "shadow of death" for a moment. Each of us has already seen his shadow or any shadow. A shadow is only a zone of darkness formed by light intercepting a body or any screen. This definition will help us better understand the phrase shadow of death in Psalm 23.

Jesus Christ is the light of the world. All who are not under His protection walk in darkness. Note that darkness in the Bible symbolizes death. When we have the light of Christ within us, and the devil wants to approach us to destroy us, our Savior, Jesus Christ, the Light that enlightens our life intercepts it. By blocking it, the Lord prevents the enemy from touching us. When we call on the Lord, He delivers and protects us by preventing the enemy from achieving his goal. The Lord bars the way to the devil and saves us from all evil. Thus, what we feel or even see is only the shadow of the devil (his works of death in our life).

The shadow of death can do nothing to you because it is not death itself but only its shadow. It can happen that death frightens us but not its shadow because what can a shadow do to us? Absolutely nothing. If we must fear someone, let us fear the One who prevents this body as a shadow from reaching us. Jesus Christ, He is the light of interception that causes the shadow. King David knew this, and that's why he said: *"When I walk in the valley of the shadow of death, I fear no evil, for You* [Jesus Christ] *are with me."* He had understood that he was not walking in the valley of death but rather in the shadow of the valley of death. No one can walk in the valley of death and live because one must be dead to enter it. However, he who walks in the valley of the shadow of death is alive because he is under the protection of the One who conquered death.

God's word declares, *"For we know that Christ since he was raised from the dead, must die no more: death has no more power over him"* (Romans 6:9). Death and all its attributes have no power over us because of Christ's sacrifice. We, therefore, need not fear anything because the Lord walks by our side. He washed away all our iniquities. So, let's walk with our heads held high and stop being unhappy. Jesus erased everything and will permanently erase our faults. If we ask Him for forgiveness, He will forgive us and cleanse us of all our sins.

My dear Grace,

"God is not a man that he should lie, or a son of man that he should change his mind. Has he said, and will he not do it? Or has he spoken, and will he not fulfill?" (Numbers 23:19). He said, "Blessed is he whose transgression is forgiven, whose sin is covered.

Blessed is the one whose sin the Lord does not count against them and in whose spirit is no deceit. You acknowledged your sin and did not cover up your iniquity." *Instead, you said to yourself: "I rebelled against the Lord; I must confess my transgressions to the Lord."*

Know that your God has indeed forgiven your sins. *"You are safe now because the Lord keeps you from trouble. Be happy under the protection He surrounds you with because you have nothing more to fear" (Psalm 32:1-7).* I would now like you, from the depths of your heart, your soul, your mind, and with the help of the Holy Spirit, to repeat these beautiful words:

"Have mercy on me, O God, according to your unfailing love, according to your great compassion blot out my transgressions.

Wash away all my iniquity and cleanse me from my sin.

For I know my transgressions and my sin is always before me.

Against you, you only, have I sinned and done what is evil in your sight. So, you are right in your verdict and justified when you judge.

Surely, I was sinful at birth.

Sinful from the time my mother conceived me.

Yet you desired faithfulness, even in the womb.

You taught me wisdom in that secret place.

Cleanse me with hyssop and I will be clean.

Wash me and I will be whiter than snow.

Let me hear joy and gladness; let the bones you have crushed rejoice.

Hide your face from my sins and blot out all my iniquity.

Create in me a pure heart, O God, and renew a steadfast spirit within me.

Do not cast me from your presence or take your Holy Spirit from me.

Restore to me the joy of your salvation and grant me a willing spirit to sustain me.

Then I will teach transgressors your ways, So that sinners will turn back to you.

Deliver me from the guilt of bloodshed, O God.

You who are God, my Savior,
And my tongue will sing of your righteousness."
(Psalm 51:1-14)

Grace, this Psalm is your 2-in-1 prayer and the Lord's answer.

May The Lord bless you.

8

The Way, The Truth
And the Life

"I am the Way, the Truth, and the Life."
~ John 14:6

Jesus Christ tells us in Matthew 11 in verse 28: *"Come to me, all who labor and are heavy laden, and I will give you rest."*

How often have you gotten up in the morning telling yourself this is the day the Lord has made? By God's grace, it will undoubtedly be better than yesterday. You have aspired to be the best, but misfortune has happened, unfortunately. You have the impression that you are no longer the same person and that something is missing from you. You cannot continue to act like everything is fine when you are not doing well.

Stop for a moment and *"examine yourself to see if you are in the faith; test yourself"* (2 Corinthians 13:5). The times we are living in are terrible, *"the hour has come for you to awake from sleep,"* (Romans 13:11)

Each one should test his actions; *then, they can take pride in themselves alone, without comparing themselves to someone else.* (Galatians 6:4-5). It is time to settle down, think, and to be able to pull yourself together.

When things do not go as expected

The past month was a nightmare; you are happy this ordeal has finally passed. Thank God, the Bible says that the blessings of the Lord are not consumed; they are new each morning. Everything will be fine now. God is faithful, and good things are yet to come. Yet a week later, you are again hit by a hard test. As if that weren't bad enough, your doctor tells you that you have cancer and nothing more can be done for you. You only have two months left to live.

- Don't worry; it's just a bad patch. This situation will eventually work out. We will fast and pray for your child all night. As long as he is in a coma, we will continue to support you in prayer. Only believe, and you will receive your miracle of healing. In a few days, your child will be discharged from the hospital. Have faith, and everything will be fine. Then, a few weeks later, your child is released from the hospital, but in a coffin.

The not-so-perfect Christian family

You've been in Christ for twenty years. Everyone appreciates you. All is well in your life, except in your home. You are in your second marriage. And precisely, your wife is about to leave you, and you have just learned that your seventeen-year-old daughter is taking drugs. You wonder how you, who are so devoted to the Lord, could have come to this. Your family problems break your heart so much that you have lost interest in life. You don't want anything anymore. You even thought about killing yourself; you are so disappointed and desperate.

How many times have you heard these words? "This year is your year!"; "The best is yet to come!"; "Only believe, and you will see the glory of God!"; "You will emerge victorious from this ordeal"; "Do not be afraid because no misfortune will reach you." "How often have you fasted and prayed without your situation changing?"

Discouraged

Your book of prophecies is complete. However, none of them has come true so far. You continue to wait, but deep down, you are discouraged and don't even believe it anymore. You now go to church more out of habit than because you have faith. Sometimes you even envy your friends and colleagues because many seem more fulfilled and happier than you. The discouragement of a monotonous life has weighed down your heart. You are alive, but spiritually you have been dead for years because you are no longer on the path of life.

Facing your true self

You have attended this church for several years, yet your life has not changed. You continue to live in the lust of this world. Everyone would like to be the pastor's right arm like you. They all envy you because they don't know who you really are. You have tried everything to get rid of your vices but in vain. You always end up falling back into sin. You know very well what the Bible says about sin, but unfortunately, you cannot free yourself from your passions. It hurts you a lot because you want it all to stop. You're tired of living in falsehood. You aspire to live a life that pleases God, but alas, you never find the strength to give up pornography and masturbation.

⁓❍⤸

Leading a double life

Everyone would love to have a family like yours. You are the ideal husband with your wife; you form the perfect couple. Besides, more than once, you have reconciled couples. Thanks to you, some of your friends are still married today. There is no finer example of Christian youth than you. Many young people come to you for advice. You are their role model. All would like to follow your example.

In your workplace, it's the best. You always make yourself available to others. You have the answers to all questions, and the word of God no longer holds any secrets from you. You are a respectful man, and your superiors trust you completely. This confidence is based on the image they have of you. You wear several masks. It depends on the person you have in front of you. Your wife, for example, knows that you are not what you appear on the outside. You have repeatedly beaten her, and you have also cheated on her with other women.

As for your computer, if it could talk... When you're out of sight, or all the lights are off, your computer screen is on, and you're watching porn videos. You masturbate in front of these videos, sometimes under the admiring eyes of your mistress, who does the same in front of her webcam. Most of your weekends, when you are believed to be on a mission or giving a lecture in another city, you are in hotels and nightclubs or on an excursion with your mistress.

In those places where no one knows you, you take your wedding ring off your finger and indulge in worldly passions. And there, nothing matters to you except to realize all your fantasies. You are ready to pay whatever it takes to make your fantasies come true. Your whole life revolves around your mistress and your sexual experiences with her. Your wife, children, Christian testimony, and even your job no longer matter when it comes to having new sexual experiences. You are, however, aware that if your double life is discovered, you will risk losing your job because it is against the ethics of the company you work for, but it is stronger than you. It is difficult for you to let go of this life. Lying is now an integral part of your existence.

Today you received this call from one of your friends in Christ who shared with you the dream he had of you last night. You know in your heart that this is a questioning message from the Lord. The message was clear: you must stop everything and change your behavior before it's too late. You could hide from the eyes of men but not from the eyes of the Lord Jesus Christ. You listened to your friend, then knelt to pray and ask the Lord for forgiveness. As soon as you finished praying, you got up and picked up your phone, but instead of texting your mistress to break up your relationship, you asked her to ensure she had booked a hotel room because it was Friday and for nothing in the world, not even for a divine interpellation you would cancel this trip.

When you left your house this Friday morning, you were aware of one thing: you had no more fear of God since your sin had reached you. It hurts you very much at first; you thought you had much in common with your lover, but in hindsight, you realize that what you have in common is a love of sin. Unfortunately for you, the wage of sin is death. Your salvation is in danger; you must react quickly because the situation you thought you could handle is trapping you. You have lost control of the situation. Only the Lord can deliver you from this grip.

The Deacon's daughter

You are the eldest daughter of one of the deacons in the church. Your father aspires to become a pastor later. You are the pride of your parents. You are held up as an exemplary role model in your family and the church. Your younger brothers and sisters follow your example. Everyone would love to have a daughter like you. However, there is one thing that those around you ignore. How will your father react if he finds out his darling daughter has a church deacon as a boyfriend? This man whose wife and children you know well. What will your younger brothers and sisters think of you if they discover this secret one day? Worse still, if they learn that you sometimes indulge in sexual orgies? Just thinking about it makes you feel bad because these are things you've never done.

You've tried to convince yourself that you're doing them out of love for the man you love and who loves you. Yet today, you have doubts about this love. Can a man who cares for you allow you to have sex with another man in his presence? Why would he share your intimate moments with another man or woman? Is this real love? Would he do the same with his wife? Will this man make you his wife one day?

Too many questions are tormenting you. How can someone who calls himself a Christian, moreover, a deacon indulge in such a level of depravity? How did you get to this stage? You had never done it in the past. This is contrary to your religious beliefs. You feel impure in the eyes of God, so dirty that you feel like you've lost your dignity. This dignity that neither gifts, money, nor even the so-called affection of this man can restore. There is still hope, even though you are on the wrong path. You must return to the foot of the cross, the only place where your dignity can be restored.

Gospel of prosperity

In your beginnings, you were one with the Holy Spirit. You only preached under His direction. You were the Lord's instrument for the salvation of souls. You were subject to His word, and the Lord was working mightily in your ministry. It could be seen by signs and wonders as it was predicted in the Bible: "And these signs shall follow them that believe; in my name shall they cast out demons, they shall speak with new tongues; they shall pick up serpents, and if they drink any deadly thing, it shall not hurt them. They shall lay hands on the sick, and they shall recover." (Mark 16:17-18)

Yes, all these miraculous signs were visible in your church. You have become a great pastor. Your church has grown and is among the largest churches in the country. You are a blessed man. However, there is one thing that takes your peace away. For quite some time, you no longer feel the presence of God by your side simply because you have turned away from the path of truth.

The love of money has taken over you. Sometimes you want to give up this life; you feel so empty. The flame that the Lord had kindled in your heart has gone out, hence the heaviness that animates you when you stand on the platform to preach. As for your messages are now under the direction of your intelligence, no longer under that of the Holy Spirit. The Lord has challenged you several times, asking you to return to your first love for Him in your beginnings. You have the desire to restore your relationship with God.

You have the desire but not the will because there are too many stakes in this return to the true gospel. You have compromised yourself so much that you are afraid to back down. And yet, this return to the truth is vital to you. You know that the message of prosperity you preach will allow you to amass wealth on this earth but will never bring you into the Kingdom of God.

Appearances can be deceiving

When we think of a strong and trustworthy Christian, we immediately think of you. There is no place you have been without leaving a good testimony. Despite your multiple trials, you remained firmly attached to the Lord without denying faith in His word. However, there is one thing you do that only God knows. This thing has become so natural to you that you no longer know how to get rid of it. The problem is that you lie a lot. As a result, you are not what people think.

You indeed love the Lord and do everything to tell the truth each time, but the lie always comes out of your mouth. You lied a lot to have the good life you have today. Your whole reputation was built on lies. Deep down, you are not proud of it because you tell yourself that "it is better to be poor than a liar" (Proverbs 19:22). You would like to get rid of this burden that distances you from God and prevents you from being filled with

His presence.

Taking shortcuts

Your home is no longer a haven of peace. Your husband, despite your best efforts, went from infidelity to infidelity. He barely spoke to you anymore. Your family is now divided: you on one side with the children, and he on his side who led the good life with other women. You are more "keeper of the house" than a wife. There is no more harmony in your relationship. This situation made you suffer a lot. You have tried everything to save your home. As a Christian, you have prayed and fasted with your sisters in Christ. You even organized meetings and prayer vigils in your house to ask the Lord to restore your marriage, but the situation did not change; on the contrary, it got worse.

You have even gone on a diet and changed your wardrobe to be more attractive to your husband, but he remains indifferent. It was in this state of discouragement and despair that one day a close friend told you that she knew someone who could help you save your marriage. She tried that person's remedy when she was in the same situation. At first, you hesitated because the word of God is clear on this, and you knew it. But unfortunately, in the end, you said to yourself, "Why not? Nothing ventured, nothing gained. It will not destroy or kill my husband; I am just trying to save my marriage by casting this spell on him."

Finally, you consulted the person who gave you his famous remedy: a bewitching potion. You followed the ritual to the letter, and since that day, your husband has completely changed. Your couple is swimming in happiness. Your husband increasingly loves you and treats you like a queen. You had become as inseparable again as when you started. The sisters in Christ you prayed with, give glory to God for answering your prayers. Your husband is transformed and has even returned to the church. Your friends give glory to God because they think He is the one who brought about this transformation. However, you know the Lord had nothing to do with this change in your husband. It was not the prayers but a spiritual bewitchment by a fetish that changed your husband. This heavy secret consumes your heart because what you have done is forbidden by God. You feel guilty: how could you, a Christian, have done such a thing?

This question keeps haunting you. You fear the consequences of your actions. You are ashamed of what you have done. So embarrassed that you no longer dare to open the Bible. The last time you did, you came across this passage: *"Let no one be found among you who offers his son or daughter as a sacrifice, who practices divination or sorcery, who engages in magic or divination, interprets omens, engages in witchcraft, casts spells or who is a medium or spirits or who consults the dead. The Lord your God abhors those who do so..." (Deuteronomy 18:10-12)*

You knew by reading this passage that it was not a coincidence but that the Lord was speaking to you. You are on the wrong path. He wants to bring you back to Him and release your pain. However, you don't know how to return because you are convinced your actions are severe. You went to seek the solution to your problems in the enemy's camp: it was a trap. As you know, sooner rather than later, you will end up reaping the fruits of this evil seed.

The Word of God is firm on this: *"God cannot be mocked. A man reaps what he sows." (Galatians 6:7)*

Christians have experienced all the situations cited above. People who, one day, had decided to make Jesus Christ their personal Savior and Lord. People who, like you and me, found themselves off the path of the truth at some point in their lives. Their story may not be like yours, but you know deep in your heart that you have a secret, just like these people. There is in your life this thing that you do and that only God knows and sees because nothing is hidden from Him. God is omniscient. In Psalm 139:1-3, King David speaking to God, says this: *"You have searched me Lord and You know me. You know when I sit and when I rise; you perceive my thoughts from afar. You discern my going out and my lying down; you are familiar with all my ways."*

As this biblical passage demonstrates, there is nothing in this world that God doesn't know. He is aware of everything we do. He masters all areas and aspects of our existence. Verse 4 of this psalm says: *"You know what I am going to say even before I say it, Lord."* So even the thoughts of our hearts are known by our God. This is something that only our Creator can do. No one in this world can know the thoughts of our hearts except God. Therefore, we cannot deceive Him or pretend before Him. We can deceive men but not our Lord, hence the importance of truthfulness in our relationship with Him. The Word of God teaches us that *"true worshipers will worship the Father in spirit and truth"* (John 4:23). We attribute this passage to times of praise and worship, but this is a mistake we all make because our whole life must be a life of worship.

Worship is a lifestyle. True worshipers are those whose every aspect of life is under the dominion of Christ. True worshipers love the Eternal God with all their heart, soul, and mind and persevere in the Lord's ways, despite their weaknesses. We must be sincere with God. It is important to let God know when something is wrong. Let's not be hypocritical with the Lord. Let's not think: "Anyway, the Lord knows that I have such and such problem, such and such weakness, so what would be the use of telling Him about it?" "He knows and sees everything!" This is not a good way to think because it will only worsen the situation.

There is a difference between trusting in the Lord and thinking that because God knows everything, it is no longer necessary to trust Him with our concerns. Indeed, the Lord is aware of everything we do simply because it is a characteristic of His divine personality. He is omniscient, omnipresent, omnipotent. Nothing can escape Him. Whether we trust Him or not, He will always know what we are doing and thinking. However, even though His nature allows Him to know everything about us, that does not justify our lack of trust in Him. The Bible urges us to *"present all our requests to the lord"* (Philippines 4:6). How do we want God to help us if we don't entrust our needs to Him?

The Lord Jesus Christ knew many of us would be burdened, troubled, and weary. This is why He made this appeal to us: *"Come unto me, all you who labor and are heavy laden, and I will give you rest."* Even though we have been Christians for years, we still carry heavy burdens. These are open doors through which the enemy can enter our lives to destroy us. To prevent this from happening, let us approach Christ Jesus so that He can relieve us of our burdens. He wants us to come to Him personally, to let Him know what's on our minds. He alone can close this door that we had opened to the devil. Without Him, we will never overcome the enemy of our soul. Sin will always camp at our doorstep as long as we live on this Earth.

The devil is watching; he exploits all the doors the Christian opens out of lust or by mistake. He will use these openings to control and subjugate the children of God. His most powerful weapon against us is sin. It is not in vain that the Lord told us: *"Watch and pray so that you will not fall into temptation. The spirit is willing, but the flesh is weak"* (Matthew 26:41). It can indeed happen that we succumb to the desires of our flesh. Everyone can have moments of weakness, but the greatest proof of love we can show to the Lord after we have succumbed to sin is to rise from our fall. *"For a just man shall fall seven times and shall rise again."* (Proverbs 24:16)

We must not enjoy or get used to sin. When we disobey His word, recognize that we have done wrong and repent. Let's not try to justify ourselves or use false reasoning; we should humble ourselves before God's mercy. He *"opposes the proud, but He gives grace to the humble"* (James 4:6). Let's not pretend that everything is fine when it isn't. Many of us are tired of wearing masks that hide our true nature. Others even blame God. Let's be honest and admit that we were disappointed when the Lord did not answer our prayers, or things did not go as expected. In my case, for example, I resented the Lord after my mother died. I wanted my mother to live. I had fasted, prayed for it, and believed God would work a miracle. But, unfortunately for me, my mother has died. I was in great pain; however, I said to myself: *"The Lord gave, and the Lord has taken away; May the name of the*

Lord be praised!" (Job 1:21)

I had quoted this verse without taking it seriously because deep in my heart, I was angry with the Lord for not having healed my mother. I no longer wanted to pray, read my Bible, or attend church. My heart was full of anger toward God. In front of people, I looked strong, but I was fragile inside. I was aware that my God saw the state of my heart, but I didn't care. Finally, one day, when I could no longer bear this situation, I approached God and entrusted myself to Him in prayer. I confessed out loud to Him that I resented Him for not acting when my mother had fallen ill and, above all, for not preventing her from dying. I asked Him to forgive me and cleanse my heart of my anger and resentment toward Him. After praying, I opened the Bible to meditate. The passage I came across that day was: *"If we accept blessings from God, we must accept trouble as well." (Job 2:10)*. It was the first time in my life in Christ that I read this passage. I understood that this message came from the Lord. After that, God filled my heart with peace, and I was set free.

Below, I will try to explain to you what happened in my life to allow you to understand what is currently happening in the life of the cases mentioned above. There are two beings: a Divine and Supreme Being (God) and a human being (Armelle).

1. Armelle was angry with God, but no one knew. Everyone thought she was a super Christian who puts everything in the hands of the Lord in times of trials. However, her anger towards God broke her fellowship with God because *"the anger of man doesn't produce the righteousness that God desires"* (James 1:20). The people around her envied her and would like to have the same attitude as her in the face of a trial. She is a fine example of the Christian faith, a model for the church. Indeed, if she dies today, she will go straight to heaven! Men cannot read other men's minds. Therefore, their testimony of Armelle is based on what she lets appear on the outside. Only God and her know that she is not true in her attitude.

2. God sees and knows everything. He holds the world and everything in it in His hands. He saw the state of Armelle's heart perfectly. He knew she was living in sin and that she would go to hell if death caught her in this state. The Lord had sent several signs to alert her, but she ignored those warnings and continued walking according to her heart's desires. She justified herself and sank deeper into sin and thus distanced herself from the Lord.

What had God done at that moment? He was silent because He had already done His part. Because of free will, He will never force us to do anything we don't want. Either way, God has nothing to gain by asking us to act on His word. On the contrary, we have much to gain from doing His will because everything He does is good. He only wishes us well. He told us this: *"I have set before you life and death, blessing and curse. Therefore choose life, that you and your offspring may live"* (Deuteronomy 30:19). You see, even with our heavenly Father, we have the right to choose between good and evil. And even though He says nothing when we choose to do the wrong thing, He knows full well that we know He sees us.

Now I would like to ask you three questions:

o Who do you think is in the better position: Armelle or God?
o Which of the two can help the other: Armelle or God?
o And finally, the last and most important question: Who should we try to please first: men of the same nature as us or God, our Creator Father?

If you answered "God" to all these questions, it means that whatever situation you are currently in, you can turn to the Lord and confide your weakness to Him. Cast all your burdens on Him. Your surroundings cannot save you. And your earthly reputation will never open the doors to the Kingdom of Heaven. It is time to take care of your salvation, whatever the price to pay: your eternity is at stake.

Stop being what you are not or even living a double life.

Accept being judged by men but approved by God because you have decided to forsake sin and walk the path of truth and life. Change your testimony in the eyes of the Lord and no longer take your relationship with Him lightly. Don't refuse to listen to Him if you hear His warnings today. Avoid deceptive reasoning and justifications; avoid being what you are not. It is time for you to unload all your secrets onto the Lord so that He purifies you, raises you from your fall, and keeps you upright. Start with telling God the truth about your life. Tell Him the whole truth, even if it is true that He already knows it. However, He wants to hear you tell Him that it's wrong, that you're not acting like children of light.

Tell the Lord :

- That you live in immorality and impurity, that your life is a lie,

- That you have shared *"the useless deeds of darkness"* (Ephesians 5:11),

- That you are ashamed to talk about what you are doing in secret and especially afraid that it will be revealed and brought to light,

- That you find your life meaningless and your life in Christ dull,

- That you are angry with Him for not having spared you this difficult ordeal and that you are lying when you say that you have placed everything in His hands,

- That you plan to leave the church and live your life outside of His word because you have been disappointed by the behavior of the pastor and some church members.

Do not hide anything from Him; open your heart so He can enter it again to restore you and replace the darkness with His marvelous light. The Bible says that God does not want the sinner's death; on the contrary, all He wants is for him to change his ways and live. It is the truth; our Father, who is in heaven, only wants our happiness. He does not want us to perish. He tells us: *"Repent! Turn away from your offenses, then sin will not be your downfall. Rid yourselves of all the offenses you have committed and get a new heart and a new spirit." (Ezekiel 18:30-31)*

The Lord continues to speak to us. Therefore *"if you hear the voice of God today, do not harden your hearts"* (Hebrews 4:7). If today, you are to be reborn again, then rise and give your life to Him for a second time. Even in the world, married couples can renew their wedding vows. It is nowhere in the Bible that you cannot renew your covenant with God. On the contrary, God Himself renews His goodness every morning. So, follow your Heavenly Father's example, pray your prayer of repentance, and make Jesus Christ your personal Savior and Lord again.

It is time to return to the feet of the cross, and *"each one examines his conduct"* (Galatians 6:4). Is this the kind of life you would like to have? Can you say without hesitation that you have nothing to hide and are proud of yourself? Nothing remains eternally hidden; even if you hide your true nature from men, you can't hide it from God. He knows you better than yourself. Have you ever read this biblical passage: *"the word has not yet come to my lips, that you already know all that I am going to say... where could I go away from you? Where can I flee from your presence?"* (Psalms 139:4-7). God controls all His creatures. You can neither run away from Him nor deceive Him. In truth, it is not men that you deceive but rather yourself because whether you like it or not, *"there is nothing concealed that will not be disclosed or hidden that will not be made known. What you have said in the dark will be heard in the daylight, and what you have whispered in the ear in the inner rooms will be proclaimed from the roofs.* (Luke 12:2-3)

Indeed, the word of God *"judges the desires and thoughts of the human heart. There is nothing in creation that can be hidden from God. In His eyes, everything is bare, uncovered and it is to Him that we all must give an account"* (Hebrews 4:12-13*).* Yes, we will be accountable to God and not to men. Therefore, it is Him and Him alone that we must fear. He alone can bring us out of the prisons we find ourselves in. He is, at the same time, our lawyer and judge. We can trust Him because He never condemns those who trust Him. Indeed that path on which you find yourself today seems luminous but believe me: this brilliance is only seen in your external being and carnal nature. Your flesh shines and looks healthy, and that's completely normal when you take care of it. But what about your spirit, your soul?

The light which currently shines on you allows you to exist and not to live. Where evil is practiced, there is no light. The devil's works are only dark, just as he is. Anyone who sins is at his service because *"you know it well: if you put yourself at the service of someone to obey him, you become the slave of the master you obey; it is either sin which leads to death, or obedience to God which leads to a righteous life"* (Romans 6:16). It is by obeying God that you will have true life. A righteous and eternal life illuminated by the true light, a light that never goes out: Jesus Christ our Lord.

You entrusted your life to Him a few months or years ago. Return to Him; He wants to bring you back to the right path. Unload on Him all your worries, weaknesses, secrets, and sorrows. He knows you've fallen and wants to pick you up. Cry out to Him with all your heart, and don't be ashamed; He will never judge

you. Invoke Him so that He comes to help you; tell
Him:

Lord Jesus Christ,

*"I don't understand why I act the way I do. For what
I want to do I do not do, but what I hate I do. And if I
do what I do not want to do, I agree that the law is
good. As it is, it is no longer I myself who do it, but it
is sin living in me. For I know that good itself does not
dwell in me, that is, in my sinful nature. For in my
inner being, I delight in God's law, but I see another
law at work in me, waging war against the law of my
mind and making me a prisoner of the law of sin at
work within me. What a wretched man I am! Lord
Jesus, you are my liberator, come and rescue me from
this body which is subject to death."* (Romans 7:15-24)

Through Jesus Christ, you can do the good you desire.
He alone can deliver you from the hold of sin that
dwells in your flesh, and He will then put you under the
control of the Holy Spirit by rekindling His flame in
your life. Do not harden your heart; above all, do not
feel condemned or judged. It is a hand of love stretched
out towards you. The Lord wants to bring you back to
His home. He wants you to change your behavior. Isn't
it Him who told you: *"I know that you have the
reputation of being alive, but you are dead. Wake up,*

strengthen what you still have, before it comes to die completely, for I have noticed that none of your actions is perfect in the sight of my God. So, remember the teaching you received and the way you heard it; be faithful to Him and change your behavior. If you don't wake up, I'll come and surprise you like a thief, without you knowing what time it will be." (Revelation 3:1-3)

Take this warning seriously; above all, do not be surprised by the Lord. I know it's not easy; you've tried many times to change your behavior and get back on the right path, and you can't. Indeed, you cannot do it simply because you are doing it alone. What you need is help. There is no better helper for your situation than the Holy Spirit. He is our guide par excellence; it is He whom the Father has sent to us so that we can accomplish His will and walk in all the truth. He has a perfect mastery of the desires of the Lord Jesus in us. Our Lord Jesus Christ is knocking at the door of your heart. He has only one desire: to come back into your life to put it in order. Do not turn down His help; above all, do not say it is too late or you have committed irreparable. With God, when it comes to your life, the irreparable does not exist. He will never let you perish if you call on Him. Don't think everything in your life is over, and you've fallen too low.

With God, we never fall too low. He will pick you up and keep you upright no matter how you fall. He has the ability and the power to get you out of any situation.

He is a limitless God to whom nothing is impossible. He told us, *"Come unto me, all ye that labor and are heavy laden, and I will give you rest"* (Matthew 11:28). It is time that you turn to Him and can finally know this rest which He speaks to you. Jesus Christ offers you a path on which there is a truth that gives life, eternal life. So, leave this dark path that leads to perdition. Get back on the right track of Jesus Christ.

The Lord speaks these words to us:

"I rebuke and correct everyone I love. So be diligent and change your behavior. Listen, I stand at the door, and I knock; if anyone hears my voice and opens the door, I will enter his house, I will have a meal with him and he with me. To those who have won the victory, I will grant the right to sit with me on my throne, just as I, after having won the victory, went to sit with my Father on His throne. Let everyone, if he has ears, listen carefully to what the Spirit is saying to the Churches! (Revelation 3:19-22)

Beloved in the Lord,

Let's take this message seriously because we are at the end of time. Undoubtedly, *"Our salvation is nearer now than when we first believed. The night is nearly over; the day is almost here. So let us put aside the deeds of darkness and put on the armor of light. Let us* behave decently as in the daytime" (Romans 13:11-13). We are sons of light, members of God's family, and therefore, a pure race. Let us not be seduced by the passions of the sons of darkness but, *"Rather, clothe yourselves with the lord Jesus Christ, and do not think about how to gratify the desires of the flesh." (Romans 13:14)*

Trust in the Lord, for He has the power to sustain us. May God sustain us all and give us the strength to persevere and stand firm in our walk with Him.

May God bless us all, and may His light enlighten our lives.

9

Children

"Train up a child in the way he should go; and when he is old, he will not depart from it."
~ Proverbs 22:6

Letter from Mark

I am a 22-year-old man, and I am the youngest of a family of four children. I grew up with Christian values and had a happy childhood with my family. Here is my problem. Today, I am in college, and as you know, there are many influences in this place of knowledge. It turns out that, for some time now, I have had more and more difficulty maintaining my relationship with God because of the new people I have been associating with.

Last week I started drinking and smoking at a party, to the point of being completely drunk. My friends tell me that it's okay to get drunk and that I should enjoy my youth. Instead of reasoning with them by talking to them about the Lord Jesus, I often prefer to keep quiet and let them convince me. Some misbehave with other students; sometimes, it happens in my presence, and I can't even react.

Yesterday while returning from class with my friends, a group of Christians spoke to us about Jesus Christ and invited us to a Bible-sharing meeting by giving us flyers. My friends laughed at them and threw the brochures on the floor. Two of them even urinated on these brochures in the presence of these young Christians. Instead of reprimanding them for their bad behavior, as a Christian, who has always respected these values, I did not say anything. The worst is that I even followed them and threw away the flyer because I was afraid and did not want my friends to make fun of me. Deep down inside, I was very ashamed of my behavior which I found genuinely unworthy of a child of God.

I want to talk to them about the Lord, but every time I try, they laugh at me, and it irritates me to the point where sometimes I end up quarreling with them out of anger. After what happened yesterday, I feel bad about myself; I repented before God and decided to respond to the Bible-sharing invitation to publicly apologize to these students that we have offended by our bad behavior. But before going there, I would like to ask my friends to change their behavior towards others because I can see they have no respect for their

103

neighbors. How to find the right words to talk to them without ending in quarrels or mockery? How should I proceed with them so that they change their behavior?

MARK.

The first word of blessing that the Lord our God addressed to man after he was created was this: *"Be fruitful and increase in number"* (Genesis 1:28). It is more than obvious; children are a blessing from the Lord. And like any blessing, we must take care of them by educating them according to the ways of the Lord. As Christians, our children must receive an education based on the word of God. The Lord does not give a blessing to serve the devil. He said, *"A man leaves his father and his mother and cleaves to his wife, and they become one flesh."* (Genesis 2:24.

The term "one flesh" also refers to one child. Other versions may use the expression "one being." Therefore, our children are the flesh born out of a marriage. These unique beings represent our heritage, a heritage to treasure. They are an inheritance we choose to reinvest in the Kingdom of God. The word of God teaches us that "Children are a gift from God; they are a reward from him." (Psalms 127:3)

One of the Lord's rewards is giving us children. These

are the fruit of our wombs. We are asked to educate them so that they may conduct themselves pleasingly in the eyes of our Lord. Every good tree bears good fruit, and for the fruit of our tree to be good, we must work to ensure that the production is perfect. One cannot want to reap good fruits from a tree that has not been taken care of or want to reap them from a plant that grows without having been carefully cultivated and which has not undergone the action of a man.

When a tree or plant grows naturally, its fruits are considered wild, hence the term "wild plants or fruits." Some fruits from this plant are toxic and poisonous because their ingestion or contact with them represents a danger for humans or animal species. In our daily life, many poisonous plants and fruits exist. However, it is not only the plants and fruits of nature that can be toxic in our daily lives. I know that what I'm about to say will shock more than one, but the fact remains that it remains a truth: the fruit of our womb can be considered a danger to his neighbor because of his behavior.

It sometimes happens because of parents who have not instilled the proper education in them, even if it is difficult to accept. Why? You will ask me, does the responsibility fall on the parents when a child misbehaves? Quite simply because it is up to the parents to *show the child the way he should follow so that when he grows up, he does not deviate from it* (Proverbs 22:6). It is the duty of parents to guide their children from an early age because; *"it is not the will of our Father who is in heaven that one of these little ones be lost"* (Matthew 18: 14). It is essential not to let the world in which we live educate our children for us. With new technologies, if we ignore them, our children can go astray. Watch the news: how many families in the United States have lost a child simply because someone else shot theirs in school? How many children get lost daily in drugs, alcohol, and video games?

Virtually every minute, young girls are being raped by a friend around the world, children are being abused and raped, and sometimes even by close friends. Even in primary schools, children are victims of physical and verbal violence from their classmates. Thus, it would not be fair to lose one's child because another parent did not educate them well. We can't let our children do whatever they want or give them whatever they ask us just because we want to please or look good to them. We must show them what is right and what is not. It is essential to set limits for them. It is possible that your child can become a danger to himself and society if you give in to every whim. The Bible says, *"That a child left to himself brings shame to his mother."* (Proverbs 29:15)

As children of God, it is up to us to instill in our children an upbringing based on the word of God. We must not conform to the modern world. If we want the fruit of our womb to produce very good fruit when ripe, it is necessary that we first lay the foundations from a young age. Later as they grow up, we will discuss all topics with them, depending on their age. We must watch over their behavior, and it is good that we do not have taboo subjects with them. Some parents, for example, refuse to talk to their children about sexuality. This is a mistake because any information we refuse to give our children will be passed down to them by today's society. The latter will take care of educating our children instead of us. We all know that the world we live in does not sort the information before sending it to us. It gives us everything it contains, whether good or bad; it is up to us to sort it out. However, to sort it, we must first select it, knowing that some contents contradict the word of God.

The world's laws are different from those of the Kingdom of God. All who live by the standards of the present century will perish. We certainly live in the world. However, we are not of the world. Therefore, we must teach our children to live according to the word of God because the jurisdiction of the Kingdom of God is based on His word, and whoever breaks the laws of it will be subject to judgment. The penalty is eternal death if that person does not repent and renounce his evil conduct. It is not a punishment we can wish on anyone, even less on our children. Hence the importance of continually teaching them the principles of God so that, later, by practicing them, they experience well-being and a long and happy life. Joseph and Mary did this when the Lord Jesus Christ was a child. The Bible tells us that "Jesus *grew in wisdom and in stature and in favor with God and man."* (Luke 2:52). Earlier in the same chapter, in verse 51, it is written that *"He obeyed them."* So even our Lord obeyed His parents when He was a child. These values had been taught to Him by them.

Nowadays, it is common to see children who do not obey their parents simply because they let them do whatever they want. If only they had disobeyed their parents! Unfortunately, this disobedience goes further: they disobey teachers and are disrespectful to other adults, which will not fail to compromise their future. It's no wonder many of them end up unhappy as adults if they don't change their behavior because the Bible is clear: If we want to enjoy a long and beautiful life, we must respect our parents. Every child owes obedience to their parents. If your children don't obey you, how can you expect them to obey the God they don't see?

It is written in the Bible that *"Children, obey your parents in the Lord, for this is right"* (Ephesians 6:1). So according to our Heavenly Father, obeying your parents is a duty, not a choice. It is a duty that must be instilled in us by our parents and that we must, in turn, teach our children from generation to generation. Our happiness depends on it: *"Respect your father and your mother is the first commandment followed by a promise: that you may be happy and enjoy a long life on earth"* (Ephesians 2: 2-3). Our happiness on this earth is partly linked to obedience to our parents. It is vital for us and our children because *"the greatest happiness of a father is to have given life to a just and wise man."* (Proverbs 23:24)

Every human being strives for happiness. We all want to attend our children's graduations and their weddings, and we also want to have grandchildren to take care of. We all want to be buried by our children, not the opposite. However, all our wishes for our children can come true if we teach them to obey God's Word. Obedience is a fundamental value for success in all plans. *"Obedience is better than sacrifice"* (1 Samuel 15:22). It assures a life full of blessings. Unfortunately, many parents do the opposite. Instead of their child obeying them, these parents are bowing to their children's four wills. They make enormous sacrifices to satisfy the desires of their children. Often, the children consider these sacrifices normal and show themselves to be more and more demanding and ungrateful. Therefore, it is not surprising that some children lose respect for their parents. Due to the lack of obedience, parents and children treat each other as equals.

There is a dysfunction in the family unit. This dysfunction has a negative impact on society. The problems that affect our community result from the family's dysfunction. This happens when we decide to do what we want instead of listening to God and obeying His word; children disobey their parents, who are disobedient to God. Parental authority is no coincidence and is not innate either. It comes from our submission and obedience to God. If we do not honor the Lord in our conduct, He who is our heavenly Father, how do we want our children to obey us when it is written that *"we are ready to punish all disobedience when your obedience is complete"* (2 Corinthians 10:6)? Let us take an example from the life of the Lord Jesus. He was completely submissive and obedient to the Eternal God. Therefore, through His obedience, we are saved and can inherit eternal life.

Man is, from his birth, hostile to obedience because he is made of flesh. We all know that *"for the desires of the flesh are against the spirit, and the desires of the spirit are against the flesh"* (Galatians 5:17), and God is Spirit, so if you *"walk in the spirit, you will not fulfill the desires of the flesh"* (Galatians 5:18). To walk in the Spirit is to obey the word of God. When we accept Jesus Christ as our personal Savior and Lord, we become children of God. This new status makes us members of the family of God. As in all families, we receive an education. This is transmitted to us through the word of God, and we must put it into practice and respect it, *"we will always find happiness if we respect the Lord our God."* (Deuteronomy 6:24)

The way the Lord disciplines us is no different from that of our parents. Moreover, the Bible says, *"The Lord your God wants to discipline you as a father disciplines his son"* (Deuteronomy 8:5). If we practice God's instructions, our children will follow ours because they will be based on the law of the Lord. Let us be good examples for our children as Christ is for the

Church. Let us always put the word of God at the center of our children's education. Even though they are Christians, many parents do not teach their children the principles of God.

The word of God is a seed that will enable children to have pure conduct and live happily as they grow. They will bear fruit. However, for this word to produce fruit, it must be regularly meditated on. It takes patience and perseverance without ever getting discouraged. We need to start instilling these values in them from an early age. The younger the children, the easier it is for us to teach them obedience.

Our children are like a vine that we cultivate. The Eternal God is the ground on which we cultivate our vineyard. He is the good ground that serves as our foundation. Then we have the water currents that cross our vineyard. Water represents the word of God. It is that word that waters our vineyard so that it produces branches and bears fruit. The winegrower represents the parent; the latter needs water even though the land is good, so his field can produce fruit. The quality of the fruit will depend on the work that the winemaker has done in the field. First, he must care for his area by creating a barrier preventing wild beasts, birds, and thieves from ransacking the seed or stealing the fruit from his vineyard. He must maintain his vine by removing weeds each time that can choke the seed. Wild beasts and birds represent the world where we live and raise our children.

The word of God must be planted in their hearts early to prevent the devil from sowing his seed in their hearts. It is fundamental to ensure that our children are rooted in the ways of the Lord so that when they grow up, they can resist the temptations of the world by using the word of God as a sword given by the Holy Spirit. As for weeds, they grow inside the field, but they are even more numerous outside the field. These are the bad habits that a child can develop. If we allow them to grow without correcting them, they will become toxic to the child. We must pull the weeds, even if it gives us much work. Weed removal is an important part of field maintenance. It refers to correcting our children by preventing them from doing what is wrong and showing them what is right. *"When we are corrected, it seems to us at the very moment that this is a cause of sadness and not of joy. But later, those who have received such correction benefit from its effect: peace associated with a righteous life."* (Hebrews 12:11)

The purpose of the correction is to bring back the rule. It enables the child to turn away from sin and disobedience. *"Rebukes and admonitions keep us on the path of life"* (Proverbs 6:23). They shape the children's character to make them like Christ. However, the correction must be made with love; otherwise, it will not bear fruit and can destroy our children's lives. As stated above, *"It is not the will of your Father who is in heaven that one of these little ones be lost"* (Matthew 18:14). Just because they are young doesn't mean they shouldn't be respected and heard. The Bible clearly says when addressing children, *"Let no one despise your youth"* (1 Timothy 4:12). Love and scolding are always associated; one does not go without the other when it comes to raising our children. Everything that is built without love does not hold. It's like building a house without a foundation. Such a house will always end up collapsing. When you correct your child without love, it is no longer correction but punishment. Punishment is the act of sanctioning by inflicting a penalty.

Correction, on the other hand, is an action that aims to make changes. Correction leads to improvement, while punishment aims at condemnation. God's discipline is not for condemnation. On the contrary, He *"disciplines us for our own good, in order that we may share in His holiness"* (Hebrews 12:10) so that *"we are not condemned with the world"* (1 Corinthians *11:32).* Correction should not be confused with punishment, which often comes from a rigid, unloving heart. Many parents bully, speak angrily, or use violence toward their children. This type of discipline has nothing to do with what the Lord recommends to us. Parents who do this end up traumatizing their children. They will fear their parents. They will obey them, not because it is correct, but because they fear being beaten or severely punished.

Others may even become rebellious because their

parents' attitudes irritate them. *"Parents do not irritate your children, lest they be discouraged"* (Colossians 3:21) but *"bring them up by correcting them and teaching them in the Lord"* (Ephesians 6:4). The phrase "in the Lord" means with love, patience, wisdom, kindness, and justice. Only by associating these qualities, which characterize the nature of God, will the upbringing we will give to our children bear fruit.

Love is the main characteristic of God. When we say that everything God does is good, it is simply because of everything He does; He does it with love. Even when He rebukes us, He does so out of love because *"the Lord corrects the one He loves"* (Hebrews 12:6). If the Lord did not love us, He would let us live as we wanted without any discipline and being carried away by every wind of doctrine. Instead, he disciplines us because He loves us. The correction here must be seen as a sign of belonging, a proof of God's love for us. Therefore, the word of God recommends us not to despise the correction of the Eternal *"for the Lord reproves who he loves, as a father the child in whom he delights."* *(Proverbs 3:12)*

Correction is essential in our relationship with God. Also, *"if you are not corrected as all His sons are, then you are not true sons but illegitimate children"* (Hebrews 12:8). If all of God's children are disciplined, why shouldn't we do the same with our children? It is necessary to discipline our children in the same way that God disciplines us. We must discipline our children. Just as God's discipline begins when we become children of God, it is good to discipline our children from an early age because the Bible says that *"foolishness clings to the heart of the child; the rod of correction will lead it away from him* (Proverbs 22:15). Foolishness here refers to a character that lacks reason and common sense.

This character must be corrected so that the child acts reasonably. You must discipline him, even if sometimes it's not pleasant. Tell yourself that, in the end, it will save him much hassle in the future. *"Do not spare the child's correction; if you strike him with the rod, he will not die. By smiting him with the rod, you deliver his soul from hell"* (Proverbs 23:13-14). Correction is, therefore, necessary since it delivers us from many evils. At first, it makes us sad, but ultimately, we are happy when we succeed. Obedience, discipline, and correction must always be part of any education if we want to live happily on this earth and later inherit eternal life. The little beatings we inflict on our children now cannot compare to their future happiness. Even our Lord Jesus Christ *"learned obedience through all that He suffered"* (Hebrews 5:8). He who was without sin, *"during his earthly life, Jesus addressed prayers and supplications, accompanied by loud cries and tears, to God who could save Him from death. And God answered Him because of His submission"* (Hebrews 5:7). Because of His submission and obedience to God, Jesus Christ *"has become the*

source of eternal salvation to all who obey Him."
(Hebrews 5:9)

Everything we do on this earth is linked to our eternity. Those who obey God will inherit eternal life, and those who do not obey the Lord will inherit eternal death.
It is the same for how we decide to raise our children. As a child of God, our main objective in bringing up our children is to save their souls from hell. This is only possible if we teach them to obey the word of God. We are to be examples of children in submission to our Heavenly Father. Sometimes words aren't even necessary if our behavior is like Jesus the Lord. Our children will follow our example more easily this way. Moreover, this will mark their character so positively that they will experience pleasure in obeying us.

The Bible says that if we believe in Jesus Christ, we will be saved, and our family as well. That does not mean my child is automatically saved because I am saved. This means that having known the bounties attached to my salvation, mainly eternal life, I will ensure that my whole family has a share in this inheritance. Also, I will teach them the benefits of obeying the word of God and being imitators of Christ. I will walk as Christ wants to impact their lives. I will teach my children the ways of the Lord so that they, in turn, can make Him their Savior and Lord. I will use all the weapons of the Spirit so that I and my household will serve the Lord. Only by doing so will our family be saved as promised in the word of God.

The Bible teaches us that a tree is known by its fruit. Thus, we will recognize our value in the behavior of our children. These are the fruit of our entrails, therefore, our production. If we are holy in our conduct, our children will also be holy because *"a good tree bears good fruit and a sick tree bad fruit. A good tree cannot produce bad fruit, nor a sick tree good fruit"* (Matthew 7:17-18). Our children will tend to do whatever they see us doing because every child likes to imitate their parents. Therefore, we must be cautious about our actions in front of our children. Our conduct must always be aimed at influencing them positively because *"the Son can do nothing by Himself; He only does what He sees the Father doing. Whatever the Father does, the Son also does"* (John 5:19). So, if we act honestly and fairly, our children will do the same. We can only teach what we know.

Our finest example in this area is Jesus Christ, our savior. His whole life, He only did what He saw His Father do. Moreover, He said that *"he who has seen me has seen the Father"* (John 14:9). Those who have known the Lord Jesus have known God the Father. He was the exact representation of the Heavenly Father. Jesus Christ, by His obedience to the Father, received all power from God because; *"as the Father is the source of life, so He has granted to the Son to be the source of life"* (John 5: 26). It was by His deeds that our Lord demonstrated the nature of Him from whom He came.

God the Father was His only source of inspiration. He lived only to follow the will of the Father. As the saying goes: "Like father, like son." Therefore, through our children, men will be able to know if we are good or bad people, hence the importance of not neglecting the education that we instill in them and our behavior towards them. We are, as parents, their first model, their source of inspiration. Let us, therefore, be good models as our Lord Jesus is for us and God the Father is for Him. When we belong to Christ, we must perpetuate the identity of God so that his glory will spread throughout the earth. However, before making Him known to the world's people, we must ensure that our family and those around us know Him first. It will be easier to spread His glory this way because we can more easily win others to Christ through our testimony and family.

The Bible asks us to conduct well so that our God will be glorified through our testimony. It is the same with our children: We can be honored or humiliated through their conduct. Their behavior depends on how well they have been trained. The values they will have will be those we have taught them. At some point in their lives, some children may stray from the right path because of bad influences. Nevertheless, these children will always return the right way because they must have received a good foundation. They will eventually realize their mistake and start on the right foot. This is what the prodigal son did when he left his father's home.

This parable is about a child who strayed from the right path at some point in his life. This son had been brought up in the ways of the Lord. However, in a moment of bewilderment, *"he indulged his desires and thus squandered all that he possessed"* (Luke 15:13). To indulge one's desires is to live in a way that is not pleasing to God. This kind of life always ends up getting us into trouble. That's what happened in this story. When he had spent all, he had, *"a great famine arose in that country."* The famine here represents the difficulties that are the consequences of disobedience. The famine was so great that the young man lacked the necessary; he could not even meet his basic needs. He, who lacked nothing in his father's house, wanted to eat the food given to the pigs. See how miserable we can be when we turn away from the presence of our Heavenly Father.

What is remarkable in this story is that the famine only occurred in the country where the young man was. In his native country, where his father lived, there was no famine. There was so much food at his father's house that all his father's servants had *"more to eat than they needed."* This young man understood this when he *"started to reflect on his situation."* It is a pity that one often realizes all the blessings in the Kingdom of God after disobeying God's word. This son returned to his senses and realized that life with his father was better than in this foreign country where famine reigned and where, despite that famine, people preferred to feed pigs instead of feeding human beings. You know, in the world, pigs are more valuable than the children of God because they belong to the world; they are in their kingdom. We must understand that the devil will always rather feed a pig that will be killed tomorrow than feed a child of God.

We are in the world, but we are not of the world. And the world knows that despite our weaknesses, we are not part of this kingdom. This young man was robbed by the children of this world. He who had been trained according to the ways of the Lord found himself lost amid the sons of darkness. After having ruined and abandoned him, these sons of darkness left him for dead; he now had to fend for himself in a famine-stricken country. But glory be to God, who never abandons His children. Even when we are unfaithful, God remains faithful.

You see, because of the upbringing he had received from his father, this son, by examining his situation, understood that his conduct was not worthy of that of a child of God. His father had educated him according to the ways of the Lord, and he knew that he was no longer on the right path and that his conduct was no longer that of a son. He had moved away from the teaching he had received from his father. This is why, realizing his mistake, he said, *"I want to go back to my father, and I will tell him: I have sinned against God and against you."* Thanks to the seed planted in his heart, this young man who had gone away returned to his father's house. He confessed that he had sinned against God.

How did he know he had sinned against God and his father? It was through the word of God that his father had taught him. He knew how a worthy son should behave. He knew he had dishonored his father with his behavior. He no longer wanted his father to consider him a son but rather one of his workers. In his father's house, everyone enjoyed good treatment: so, it is with all who belong to God.

This parable shows us that whatever we teach our children is never lost. A child of God who repents his evil works will be saved. The good seed always ends up bearing good fruit. Our children will never forget the teaching they received. Even if they rebel, they eventually return to their senses and the right path. The father of this young man trusted in God. He knew the Lord would watch over his son. When the latter returned home, his father ran to meet him and rejoiced in his return. He made no unpleasant remarks to his child. On the contrary, he said: *"My son here was dead and has come back to life, he was lost, and I have found him."*

God is faithful and will not let our children get lost in this world. Therefore, our only responsibility is to instill in them the laws of God when they are young. Then, the Lord will take care of them and cause his divine seed to germinate in them so that they, in turn, will be God-fearing people and, therefore, good parents.

Dear Mark,

"If sinful men entice you, do not give in to them. If they say come along with us; let's line in wait for innocent blood, let's ambush some harmless soul, do not go along with them, do not set foot on their paths; for their feet rush into evil; they are swift to shed blood." (Proverbs 1:10-11)

You know Mark, *"don't quarrel wantonly with someone who hasn't done anything to you. Do not envy violent people and do not imitate their conduct. For the Lord hates those who turn away from Him, but He gives His friendship to the upright"* (Proverbs 3:30-31). Indeed, it is only by observing the word of God that the young man can keep pure conduct. So, the solution to your problem is in your Bible.

You said that *"from your childhood, indeed, you have known the Holy Scriptures; they can give you wisdom. "For all scripture is inspired of God and helpful in teaching truth, refuting error, correcting faults, and forming a righteous way of life"* (2 Timothy 3:15-16). However, if you want the word of God to work entirely in you, *"flee the passions of youth; seek*

122

righteousness, faith, love, peace with those who call on the Lord with a pure heart. But reject crazy and stupid arguments: you know they produce quarrels. And the lord's servant must not be quarrelsome but must be kind to everyone, able to teach, not resentful.

Opponents must be gently instructed in the hope that God will grant them repentance leading them to a knowledge of the truth, and that they will come to their senses and escape from the trap of the devil, who has taken them captive to do his will. (2 Timothy 2:22-26)

You are young, and it is normal for you to want to enjoy your youth but do so in line with the upbringing you received from your parents. Do not seek the approval of your friends but rather that of God. Remember that *"the Lord knows his own, and whoever claims to be of the Lord must turn away from evil" (2 Timothy 3:19).* Pull yourself together and enjoy your youth while having conduct that glorifies the Lord your God.

May the Lord Jesus Christ be your reference.

10

Devotion to God

"Teach me your way, Lord, that I may remain on your faithfulness; give me an undivided heart, that I may fear your name."
~ Psalms 86:11

One day, Jesus Christ sent seventy-two disciples on a mission. Before they left, He told them, *"The harvest is great, but the laborers are few. Pray therefore to the lord of the harvest to send out laborers into his harvest"* (Luke 10:2). Two thousand years have passed since that day. Yet, despite the prayers and the number of workers increasing daily, the Lord's Church still needs workers. But unfortunately, we also see that a particular type of worker is disappearing from the Church: pious workers.

In our daily lives, we engage in several activities necessary for our development, that of our family in our work, or for health reasons. In addition, we do activities with joy and others under duress. These activities can be imposed on us by the environment we belong to or because we want to imitate those around us to obtain certain favors. Sometimes it is just because we do not want to appear different from others.

Most of the time, pursuing social success drives us to act this way. It is not a bad thing to seek success in life; on the contrary, we should all aspire to a better life because that is what God wants for us, that we can be successful in all our endeavors. However, what is not right is to seek success above all and at all costs and to put God below or outside our success. Indeed, the world we live in is a world of compromise.

Many Christians have been led to act against their convictions to obtain a contract or a social position or to be successful. These people have indeed succeeded and are very successful. But at what cost? At the cost of their golden soul, *"what good is it for someone to gain the whole world and yet forfeit their soul?"* (Mark 8:36)

The Lord has promised to make us successful in this world. The Bible says that "with *God we will gain the victory"* (Psalm 60:12). Doing feats automatically generates success. Achievement and success are, therefore, part of God's plans for our lives. What is not part of God's plan for our life is to gain the world and lose its soul in the process of our success. Don't confuse success with popularity.

A popular person attracts the public and the media's attention. This word comes from the adjective famous, which means "many, famous, illustrious" or "who is celebrated." We must celebrate God alone and not seek to be celebrated. It is by winning the world that one becomes famous, and this most often involves certain sacrifices and renunciation, as the letter below testifies.

Letter from a celebrity

I am writing to you today because I find myself at an impasse. I am "at a crossroads," as they say. In front of me, there are two paths. I must decide and can't move forward if that decision isn't made. It all started as a game. At first, I tried to refuse by reasoning with those who pushed me to act this way, but all my attempts failed.

They remained firm on their position (they had the power and the means, and I only had my talent). They made me understand that others before me had been there, and that's how their world works. It was the price to pay to succeed and be successful. They convinced me (I was blinded by the urge to succeed) that my talent alone was not enough to make me succeed and be successful, that I could succeed, but I would not go far because big contracts require certain sacrifices. What I refused to do now; I would end up doing it tomorrow if I wanted to succeed in this field.

I remember they told me that I didn't have enough rage in me (the rage of the glory of this world); that's what made me hesitate, according to them. They gave me time to think about it and asked me to contact them if I changed my mind. They added that it was not them but me who needed their help and that thousands of people like me in the country dream of having a single opportunity to meet people like them.

On leaving their house, they gave me a brochure in which all the famous people who had used their services to reach the height of glory appeared. I started thinking and told myself that I needed this contract, that it would open the doors to success and glory for me, and that, as they had told me, I was not the first and would not be the last. Others before me, including Christians like me, have gone this route.

The Lord indeed condemns such practices, but it's not every day that I will do it, just once or twice. Then I will ask Him for forgiveness. This contract was going to change my life. I couldn't let such an opportunity pass. I had suffered too much and worked too hard to reach this level. This was the opportunity of my life.

Instead of praying, I reasoned (maybe I didn't want to pray because I knew that this path was not the one the Lord wanted me to take, He, who had given me this talent, did not want me to compromise myself to

128

succeed). After careful consideration, I contacted them. I submitted to their demands and signed this contract. Today, I am famous and very successful. I received several awards; I am known in my country and worldwide. People talk about me in all the media and newspapers.

Many people envy me and would like to experience the same success as me. They don't know that there is a place I wish I had been nominated for and a person from whom I wish I had received the greatest award a man could receive. This place was heaven. Unfortunately, I am not known to anyone there because my name does not appear in any register. So, I cannot be rewarded by God. Men reward success, but God rewards faithfulness. I was not faithful to God, and it was at the cost of my soul that I became famous.

Some will tell me I had no choice because that's how this environment works, but that didn't prevent me from loving God. Moreover, each time I appear in the media, I talk about my faith and how, thanks to Him, I have reached such a level of success. However, this is a lie because my success does not come from the Lord, and I had to end my relationship with Him to be what I am today.

I completely agree that this is how this environment works. It was repeated to me several times. However, when it came to choosing, believe me, I had a choice.

They didn't force me to do anything. The truth is that I preferred success to remaining faithful to the Lord, knowing that with God, I could also experience success. I didn't want to wait; I couldn't wait for the big hit. If the Creator of Heaven and Earth Himself gives us a choice, then we can necessarily choose before men.

Today, I must make a more difficult choice. Before, when I still had nothing, it was easy to choose, but now with everything I own and the fame I enjoy, it's not easy. I must choose between two types of life:

1. The first life gives me success and all the glory that goes with it. I can conform to the present century and all its desires.

By choosing this life, I resolve to be alive in this century but dead in the century to come.

2. Regarding the second life, it forbids me to conform to the present century and all its desires. Instead, I must live under the direction and dominion of the Spirit of God.

By choosing this life, I take the firm resolution to be dead in the present century but alive in the century to come. What should I decide when we know that the first century will end one day with all covetousness and the second century will last forever? Choosing the second life will mean giving up everything I have. This is very difficult for me because I am attached to my possessions. What should I do? Give up and live or stay and die?

ANONYMOUS.

It is possible to be in any social or professional setting and remain devoted to God. Unfortunately, Christians today are very much in keeping with the present age, seeking men's approval, not God's. Others are even difficult to identify among those who are not Christians simply because they behave like them. If the Lord allows us to frequent worldly circles, it is not to act like them but so that through us, those who are not Christians have *"the possibility of changing their behavior and receiving true life"* (Acts 11:18). This true life that is found nowhere else but in Jesus Christ.

Never submit to demands that go against what the word of God declares. The salvation of your soul is worth more than any privilege, position, or wealth in this world. Prophet Daniel and his friends understood this principle when they were at the service of King Nebuchadnezzar. These young men remained steadfast and faithful to their God, and by their attachment to God, the king and all his entourage recognized that the God of Daniel was above all gods and all rulers. What was the secret of Daniel and his companions to preserve their faith while serving a king as formidable and powerful as Nebuchadnezzar?

Daniel and his friends, like several heroes of the Bible, had devotion to God as their secret. They had absolute confidence in the Lord; they submitted to him in everything and for everything. Their faith in God was unshakable. There was a direct connection to the Kingdom of God in everything they did. They were not distracted by the pleasures indulged in by all who had access to the court of the king of Babylon. They served the king without worshiping the various gods of the Babylonian people. It was difficult for them to stay firmly attached to their God in an environment where people had one or multiple gods, mainly when serving a king who thought he was a god and could kill everyone who did not submit to his demands. They had not tried to convert the Babylonian people and even less the king (it was not their mission). They had not even attempted to build a temple for their God in Babylon, even though they had been deported there. They couldn't control people who didn't believe in their God. The only thing they did in Babylon was to continue being devoted to the one and only true God: The Eternal God.

We must all adopt this attitude, regardless of the environment in which we find ourselves. It is not for us to conform to the gods of this world or some unhealthy demands of those around us. If anyone must change sides, it will never be us because our God is the only true God who sacrificed His only son so that we may have eternal life. The riches, popularity, and glory you will have on this earth can never compare to such a sacrifice and the promise that goes with it. Therefore, never sin against the Lord to please a person, not even yourself. Avoid justifying yourself or reasoning with someone who asks you to do something against God's word.

In this world, you can only control your dedication to God. If you manage to control the latter, then nothing and no one on this earth can compromise you. Moreover, you will prosper in all respects just as the state of your soul prospers.

The Lord Jesus knew this, and that is why He told us: *"But seek first his Kingdom and his righteousness; and all these things shall be added onto you"* (Matthew 6:33). What did He mean by everything else? The rest here are the things that concern us every day: having a good job, starting a family, owning a house, a car, succeeding in this campaign, being well dressed, having a lot of money, health... in one word, to be successful in our businesses. However, the Lord says that all these concerns should be secondary. Our main concern should be the Kingdom and the practice of God's righteousness. Let's not be like the pagans because they are *"the ones who are constantly looking for all this"* (Matthew 6:32). The Lord warns us against attachment to all that is earthly and temporal. These are riches which *"worms and rust destroy, of which burglars break open the locks to steal"* (Matthew 6:19). They have nothing to do with the goods you accumulate in the Kingdom of Heaven.

No one can steal this wealth from you because it is imperishable and eternal. There are many benefits to obeying God and practicing His righteousness. This is what the book of Daniel teaches us. If you feel your faith weakening or are in a situation where you are being asked to compromise, open your Bible, and read the book of Daniel. If you don't have your Bible when someone makes this indecent offer to you, it doesn't matter! Just look up Daniel's or Joseph's story on the internet on your cell phone. As you read their story, you will see they faced the same problems as we do today. The Bible says that Daniel and his friends were selected based on certain criteria: they *"must have no physical defects; they were to have good appearance and be filled with wisdom, knowledge and discernment"* (Daniel 1:5). In addition to these criteria, they were all from royal families or noble families. However, all these criteria did not prevent them from being consecrated to God and leading a life of piety. However, they were in the service of a formidable king who had the right of life and death over all the inhabitants of his kingdom.

King Nebuchadnezzar spread terror in all the kingdoms of his day. He had destroyed the temple in Jerusalem that King Solomon had built in the year 587 BC. He had taken to Babylon *"some of the sacred vessels of the temple of God"* (Daniel 1:2). Therefore, it was almost impossible to resist him because he killed anyone who dared to oppose him or did not meet his expectations. He even sometimes demanded outrageous things from those in his service, such as revealing the content and the meaning of a dream he had had that troubled him. Can you imagine the extent of his request? Here is a man who had a dream which disturbed him and who, upon waking up, no longer remembers what he dreamed of. This man will then summon these soothsayers to tell them this: *"I had a dream that troubled me a lot. I would like you to tell me what that dream was about."* (Daniel 2:3)

This request was beyond the abilities of his servants and any human being. How can you reveal to someone a dream that he had, and he can't even remember on top of everything? His servants answered him, saying, "Your Majesty, *no human being in the world can do what you require"* (Daniel 2:10). They added that "no *king, however powerful, had asked such a thing of a divine."* The king nevertheless refused to listen to reason. He got angry and decided they would be cut into pieces if these servants did not tell him about the dream and its explanation.

From this story, we can see how often Nebuchadnezzar was dangerous and why all feared him. When he got angry, he inflicted on his subjects very harsh sentences. This is why no one dared to resist or stand up to him. Here is a short description of Daniel's boss and his friends. I don't think you or I have ever dealt with this kind of person. Let's say we are fortunate; this was not the case for all who served the king. Whenever this king asked the people to do things contrary to the law of the Lord, Daniel, and his friends refused to submit to the king, even if it would cost them their lives. Thus, these young men remained firmly attached to the Lord despite their trials and persecutions. Even when they had attractive offers, they did not compromise. They had taken the firm resolution not to become impure, which they did.

Today, devotees like Daniel and his companions are on the way out. We almost look for them in churches. There are undoubtedly many workers, but few are devoted to God in this way. Devotion is the state of mind of a dedicated person to God. The Holy Spirit controls this person's thoughts and feelings. We cannot be devoted to the Lord if we do not pray, if we do not meditate on His word if we do not obey Him, or if we yield to our every inclination. In one word, devotion to God is nothing but consecration. We must have a real personal relationship with God.

To know the One we believe in, we must spend time secretly with Him. Our spirit must be connected to His Spirit. He must occupy not only the first place but all other places in our life. In our life, after God, it must still be God and always God. Others must conform to the Lord's position in our lives, not the other way around. God must be our priority. Everything else must come after Him. God deserves that we render Him the honor and the glory that are due to Him and that we have for Him an ardent love. Nothing and no one should cause us to sin against Him. Everything we do should relate to the Kingdom of God. Regardless of times and circumstances, it is good to maintain an attitude worthy of true worship. We should never have a second plan apart from God's plan for our life.

Faced with those who want you to compromise, stand firm and do not try to justify yourself. Act like Shadrach, Meshach, and Abednego, who stood up to King Nebuchadnezzar by refusing to worship the golden image he had erected. Instead, they preferred to die remaining faithful to God rather than live by obeying the king. The king was so angry at their refusal that he threatened to throw them into a furnace with intense fire. However, the king was so sure of himself and his power that before throwing them into the fire, he asked them the following question: *"What god could then snatch you from my power?"*

Despite this threat, Daniel's friends did not change their position. Instead, they replied to the king in these terms: *"Majesty, we do not want to try to justify ourselves. Know, however, that our God, the God we serve, can save us; yea, He will deliver us out of the furnace and out of your power"* (Daniel 3:16-17). Their response to the king shows how much they trust in God.

They trusted Him so much that they knew He could get them out of any situation. What struck me the most when reading this story was what they added in verse 18. Listen to their response: *"And if He does not,* (may God not deliver them from the fiery furnace), *know well that we will still refuse to serve your gods and to adore the golden statue that you have erected."* So, they decided to remain faithful to Him even if the Lord did not save them from the fiery furnace. Their love for the Lord did not depend on what God did or could do for them. They loved the Lord for what He was: the Unique and True God.

They knew that the law of God was above all laws. And precisely, this law they knew by heart said this: "Thou *shalt worship no other gods but me. Thou shalt not bow down before such statues, thou shalt not worship them"* (Exodus 20:3,5). Thus, it was almost impossible for these young people to obey the king because their God was above the king and all authority. So, they preferred to die rather than worship other gods. They were finally thrown into the fiery furnace. The latter was so hot that the flames killed even the soldiers throwing them there. The Bible says that the three friends felt bound in the heart of the furnace, but they were not killed by fire because the Eternal had sent an angel to deliver them. They came out of the fire untouched and did not even have the smell of burning!

On the verge of amazement, the king exclaimed, *"Thank you to the God of Shadrach, Meshach, and*

Abednego! He sent his angel to deliver his servants who, full of confidence in him, disobeyed my royal command. They preferred to expose themselves to torture rather than serve and worship other gods than their own" (Daniel 3: 28). Isn't it wonderful to see that the one who asked God's faithful followers to compromise is the first to bear witness to the power and the magnificence of the Lord? He, who at first thought that their God was incapable of delivering them from his power and manifesting his power, finally confessed that no god could accomplish such deliverance.

This story testifies to the faithfulness of God, who never abandons those who are full of confidence in Him and who do not turn aside from His law. Indeed, Daniel's friends relied on the law of the Lord to resist the king. They remained attached to this law thanks to their faith in God. In the book of Ephesians, the apostle Paul recommends, *"Always take up the shield of faith with which you can extinguish all the flaming darts of the evil one"* (Ephesians 6:16). There is nothing in this world that faith in God cannot do. What is impossible with men is possible with God. However, this possibility only arises when one firmly believes in God through absolute obedience and there is no doubt in the heart. Doubt is the biggest killer of faith that exists in this world. Never doubt. Even when doubt wants to settle in your heart, repel it with the power of the name of Jesus Christ.

A faith like that of Daniel and his friends is maintained by a life of sanctification. Their daily exercise was piety. An exercise that keeps you in the presence of God and helps you stay away from evil because *"Physical training is good, but training for godliness is much better, holding promise for both the present life and the life to come"* (1Timothy 4:8). Godliness is that characteristic of sanctification that enables us to live by remaining faithful to our Almighty Father, by submitting ourselves to His authority. This is not an attitude that is acquired overnight. It requires us to practice it every day. It is a spiritual exercise to which we submit not our body but our spirit and soul. Also, to have the capacity and the strength to train ourselves without being discouraged, we must take the Holy Spirit of God as a coach because no human trainer can guide us in this exercise, not even ourselves.

God is Spirit; it is impossible for us to love Him with all our heart, with all our soul, and with all our mind without the action of the Holy Spirit because *"the love of God is poured out in our hearts by the Holy Spirit"* (Romans 5:5). We cannot submit to the perfect will of God with our flesh or by our efforts. There will always be a big difference between what we do with our efforts and what we do with the Holy Spirit. The works of the Spirit are invisible and eternal; those of the flesh are visible and temporal. Thus, godliness with the action of the Spirit of God will teach us to *"forsake evil conduct and earthly desires, and live a reasonable, righteous life in this world, faithful to God"* (Titus 2:12-13). If we are not serious about our fellowship with God, it will be difficult for us to remain faithful to Him and resist the temptations of this world. Being serious is not just about believing by faith alone. It is also about praying and leading a righteous life. Prayer is a powerful weapon for all who want to remain in sanctification. It is by praying that we receive revelations from God. We dismantle all our enemies ' plans through prayer in the precious name of our Lord Jesus Christ. It is by praying that the young people will have dreams and the old men visions, according to what chapter 2 of Joel: 28 says: *"I will pour out my Spirit on all flesh, your sons and your daughters will prophesy, your old men will have visions and your young people will have dreams."*

Any Christian, without exception, can live this prophetic word if he wishes because we have all received the same Spirit. Knowing all that the Spirit of God can do in us is enough for us to be attentive to His voice and follow His directives; that is how we can become successful. Sanctifying life is only possible under the guidance of God's Holy Spirit. Consecration to God is the primary condition for winning great battles.

The Bible teaches us that nothing is impossible with God. Repeating it is not enough; we must believe in it and be in the conditions that will allow us to experience it. This was what Daniel had understood when he was in the service of Nebuchadnezzar. This king asked his servants to tell him the dream he had had the night before and demanded that they interpret it. The other servants had told the king that no one in this world could fulfill such a request. They were telling the truth. Yet the king did not want to hear anything and decided to put all the wise men of Babylon to death, including Daniel and his companions. When Daniel learned of the decree of execution, he went to the king; he wanted King Nebuchadnezzar to grant him enough time to tell him about the dream and its interpretation. Daniel did not react like the other wise men because he knew his God could reveal this dream even if the king's request was excessive.

What is impossible to man is possible with God. Daniel was a young and devoted servant of God and was in the best position to reveal the dream to the king. The word of God declares: *"Call unto me, and I will answer you, and I will tell you great things, hidden things, which you do not know"* (Jeremiah 33:3). He had only one option: to pray that the God of heaven would reveal to him the king's dream. He did, and the Lord revealed the dream and its explanation. This mystery was revealed to Daniel because he lived a blameless life before God and had unwavering confidence in Him. Our attachment to God will always make the difference between the people of this world and us, regardless of our environment, because we are sons and daughters of light. The Bible is full of stories of people who remained faithful to God despite being in the service of an authority that worshiped foreign gods and idols. Through their devotion and the wonders God worked through them, the kings, and authorities they served had no choice but to recognize their God as the One and True God. The children of light are destined to enlighten the world by doing not ordinary things but extraordinary things. This is what our Savior Jesus Christ wanted us to understand when He spoke in these terms: *"Let your light shine before men, that they may see your good works, and glorify your Father who is in heaven"* (Matthew 5:16). So, everything we do in this world must be to honor and glorify our God.

Our achievement and success must always ensure that it is God and only Him who is celebrated, not us. That's what happened with Daniel. After Daniel recounted the dream and gave his explanation, King Nebuchadnezzar bowed face down and paid homage to Daniel and said to him, *"Truly your God is the greatest of all gods, and the lord of kings. He alone reveals the mysteries since you were able to reveal this mystery to me"* (Daniel 2:47). The evil which the devil desired to do to Daniel and his friends by having them killed in a fiery furnace was changed to good by the Lord. The Lord took an ordinary young man like Daniel to do something extraordinary and confound the king and his seers. Even when they sought to kill him out of jealousy, they failed. Even though they all served the king, Daniel had decided not to defile himself. He led a godly life.

Therefore, *"they could find no fault or failing, for he was perfectly honest: there was really nothing against him"* (Daniel 6:5). Not only did they find no sin in Daniel, but they recognized that he surpassed them all in his exceptional abilities because he possessed *"an exceptional mind, discernment, intelligence, and ability to explain the dreams, deciphering riddles, and solving problems"* (Daniel 5:12). Thus, if like Daniel, we live in sanctification, it will be difficult for men or our enemies to reach us and be able to corrupt us.

The Bible says that they will make war on us, but they will not overcome us because, by our faith in Jesus Christ, our victory is assured in advance when we maintain our communion with Him alive. Intimacy with God is a fortress of protection against the lusts of this world and a safe place to be invincible. The Spirit that was in Daniel is the same that is in us today. It's the Holy Spirit of God. As a child of God, we all need to understand that it is not just any spirit that God has put in us. It's a Spirit as Holy as He that gave it to us. This Spirit can only subsist in a holy environment. Anything impure limits His effectiveness. It cannot manifest fully when we are not in agreement with God. To agree with God, we must like Him and be holy in all our conduct. Because of our human nature, it is impossible for us to live in holiness. God sent us the Holy Spirit, so we would have the power to do His will. It is through Him that the power of God is manifested in us. It is the promise that our Lord Jesus made to us before ascending to heaven: *"You will receive power, the Holy*

Spirit" (Acts 1:8). Thus, He *"is not a Spirit of fear given to us by God, but a Spirit of strength, love and wisdom."* (2 Timothy 1:7)

All the characteristics of God are present in His Spirit. It is to act fully in us that God has given us so that we may have all His capacity within us. It was the Spirit of God who revealed the king's dream and its interpretation to Daniel. As a human being, Daniel couldn't do so. He and his friends had to implore *"the mercy of the God of heaven concerning this mysterious dream, lest he be executed with the other wise men of Babylon"* (Daniel 2:18-19). You must approach the Lord to understand how almighty and full of goodness He is. By having a personal relationship with Him, we come to live His promises. It is by spending time in His presence that one achieves prosperity in all respects, as it is written in 3 John 1: 2: *"Beloved, I pray that in all respects you may prosper and be in good health, just as your soul prospers."* This verse teaches us that we should first prosper in our spiritual life. Prosperity, in all aspects, is conditioned by the prosperity of the soul.

A prosperous soul delights in fortifying itself in the presence of God. Therefore, we must first be successful in our spiritual life with our Heavenly Father. Then we can experience success in all other areas of our lives. The quality of our relationship with the Lord will determine our level of success on earth. If we find that we are struggling to succeed in our endeavors or that there is an area of our life that is always in eternal restart or non-fulfillment, we should first question our relationship with God. The Christian life consists of having quality time with God. If we don't take time in secret with our God, it's only natural that we can't be successful in our endeavors.

The Lord never blesses us halfway. When He blesses us, He does so in all areas of our lives. A Christian should not say: *"I am blessed in my professional field, but at the marital level, it is hell! The blessing* of the Lord is always total and never followed by any sorrow. If your blessing is followed by sadness, it is not from God. The Lord's blessing comes through obedience to His word and righteousness. We cannot cheat or compromise to get something and then say that the Lord has blessed us. The Bible says, *"Unless the Lord builds the house, their builders labor in vain"* (Psalm 127:1). Everything that the Lord builds has a solid foundation and stands forever. It is, therefore, important to develop our projects under the direction of the Holy Spirit if we want them to have the expected success. God is Spirit, so all our enterprises, even the most insignificant, must first be built in spirit and truth, in secret with God, in His presence during our moments of prayer and worship. Whatever we haven't seen in spirit, in intimacy with the Lord, we won't get.

Before being accomplished in the real world, everything is first accomplished in the spiritual world. With God, chance does not exist. What the Lord has not given us cannot be considered a blessing because there is a big difference between what we achieve with our strength and intelligence and what we achieve with the Spirit of God. The works of God are permanent; they bear fruit in abundance and in all seasons. As for the works of men, they are ephemeral, and their production is limited. Let's not try to get things with our strength and then ask the Lord to bless them. God cannot bless what He has not approved. When we refuse to wait on the Lord, we act this way and become impatient with our projects' outcomes. We create blessings for ourselves that we attribute to God. We implore the Lord to get us out of trouble when we face difficulties. And if God does not answer our cries, we say He has abandoned us. God never leaves His children. Instead, his children turn their backs on Him by refusing to do His will.

God remains faithful to Him, even when we are unfaithful to Him. He never breaks His covenant with us; we find it difficult to be faithful to Him. We go back and forth: sometimes, we are with Him, and sometimes we go elsewhere. Even when we turn from His path, God still leaves His door wide open behind us to allow us access to Him should we decide to return to Him. We must understand that God's faithfulness has nothing to do with us. For example, a woman must be faithful to her husband and vice versa. In case of infidelity, one of the spouses can ask for a divorce.

God's faithfulness is different. God does not owe loyalty

to men. It is instead to His word that He owes fidelity. That's why God remains faithful no matter how we behave, how bad our sins are, or the difficulties we face, in good times and bad. Whether we are faithful or not, He sticks to His word. Circumstances should not make us unfaithful. We must be consistent in our attachment to God. Daniel's friends had the same attitude as God when they decided to remain faithful to Him because they were themselves faithful to God. They were able to affirm with conviction to Nebuchadnezzar that: *"the God whom we serve is able to save; yea, He will deliver us out of the furnace and out of your power."* (Daniel 3:17)

The Lord did exactly what they said: He delivered them from the fiery furnace because He knew they were His faithful ones. *"The Lord loves the rule of law, and He does not abandon His faithful ones"* (Psalm 37:28). When our conduct pleases Him, He smooths our paths so we can move boldly through life. Our relationship with God must be based on His word, which does not change and never will. Jesus Christ, our Savior, had already warned us in these terms: *"Heaven and earth will pass away, but my words will never pass away"* (Matthew 24:35). So, if the word of God does not change, neither can He change. If we obey His word, we will experience the benefits of His faithfulness throughout our lives. Some people interpret the word of God to their advantage, while others obey what suits them and ignore or justify what condemns them. For example, a person once told me that when someone hurts him, he uses the Old Testament and obeys the verse that says: *"Thou shalt cast no pity look, eye for eye, tooth for tooth, hand for hand, foot for foot"* (Deuteronomy 19:21). This person, like most Christians, lives under the New Covenant. However, several aspects of his life fall under the Old Covenant.

A Christian who desires to please God cannot circumvent the word of God to his advantage. The sacrifice of Jesus Christ on the cross calls us to walk in the newness of life according to the Spirit. If the Spirit leads us, we are no longer under the law. God watches over His word and respects His covenant with us. He always honors His commitments; He always accomplishes everything He says. If we are not answered, it is simply because we have not respected our part of the contract. Every *"worker deserves his wages"* (Luke 10:7). Why do we want to receive a salary for work we have not done? If we do our part, the Lord will reward us; there is no better master than Him. He has promised us great rewards if we remain faithful to Him. Even if His promises for us are slow to be fulfilled, do not be discouraged; trust Him because *"God is not a man that he should lie"* (Numbers 23:19). He always does what He says. Even if it tarries, let us faithfully await the blessing that the Lord has promised us. Let's stay on the path of its accomplishment and avoid taking shortcuts that will take us away from our destiny. Whatever opportunity presents itself to us, there will be no point in seizing it if it is not in accordance with the principles of our Heavenly Father.

Just as *"all things work together for good to those who love God"* (Romans 8:28), all things that are not according to the word of God work together for the misfortune of those who are not faithful to God. Therefore, anyone who wishes to succeed and live happily on this earth must, like Daniel, be devoted to the Lord. Indeed, Daniel's enemies tried to bring him down by issuing a decree that said, *"Whoever within thirty days prays to any god or man, except [the] king, shall be thrown down "into the lion's den"* (Daniel 6:7). However, this decree did not change Daniel's schedule, he continued to pray and worship his God three times a day.

The Bible says that when he heard of the decree, Daniel *"retired to his house, where the windows of the upper room were open toward Jerusalem"* (Daniel 6:10). He knelt to pray and praise his God, as he usually did. Despite the decree, he did not even hide to invoke his God. For Daniel, it was clear that nothing could prevent him from respecting his prayer times. He could have told himself that, during the thirty days, he would pray with the windows closed so that no one would see him. But he didn't change his way of doing things. On the contrary, he honored his God. The rest of the story we all know. Daniel was thrown into the lions' den, and his God, whom he served with dedication and perseverance, snatched him from the lions' claws. Some people tend to compare themselves to Daniel in the lion's den when they are in a hostile environment, are persecuted in their workplace, or face specific discrimination. However, it is sometimes difficult to know if they are like Daniel in the lion's den or if they are just lions. Because, you know, in the lion's den, there are only two possibilities to escape the lion's mouth.

The first is that of Daniel; thanks to our faithfulness to God, He will send an angel to shut the mouths of the lions so that they do us no harm. In this situation, the other possibility of deliverance is to be a lion yourself because a lion cannot eat another lion. In this case, the Lord does not intervene because the lions recognize you as one of them. This is not a judgment, but many Christians who have allowed themselves to be corrupted by the present century do not realize they have already become lions. Therefore, lions no longer need to devour them. If, without the intervention of God, we become invincible in the face of our enemies, it means that we have the same nature as those we think are our enemies. And suppose we are of the same nature. In that case, it is impossible that we can fight against each other because, as the word of God says: *"Any kingdom divided against itself will be ruined, and a house divided against itself will fall. If Satan is divided against himself, how can his kingdom stand?"* (Luke 11:17-18*)*

The Lord will never turn us into a lion or a flame to save us. He will always send an angel to protect and serve us as He did for Daniel and his friends, Jesus in the desert, and several biblical characters. To be like Daniel in the lion's den, we must stand firm in our relationship with God. No matter the difficulties, as Christians, we must trust God and remain faithful to Him because whatever the adversity, our perseverance and devotion to God will always bring us victory. It is unshakable faith in God that moves mountains. Our faith in God must allow us to refuse the world's offers. We don't have to turn into lions to live with the lions of this world. We must cling firmly to God because He will protect us amid this world's lions and the flames of fire. Our enemies may lay traps for us to try to bring us down or to compromise us. However, if we keep our eyes fixed on the Lord, we can avoid all the pitfalls that lie in our way. Even if we fall, the Lord will lift us. No matter how many times we fall, how hard or how badly we fall, or where we fall, the Lord always raises His faithful ones. With God, there is always hope. The only thing we must do is trust Him and dwell in His presence. If we don't know God, it will be difficult for us to serve Him and be faithful to Him because the knowledge of the Lord enables us to stand firm in the face of adversity and triumph over our enemies. Did he not say, *"My people perish for lack of knowledge"* (Hosea 4:6)? The Bible says that *"those of the people who know their God will firmly resist."* (Daniel 11:32)

Seek first the Kingdom and the justice of God, it is to seek first to know God, to focus our attention on Him, to make Him our priority. It is by knowing God and by seeking to know Him that we will be able to get all that we desire above all else because God *"deny nothing good to those who walk in integrity"* (Psalm 84:12) and *"those who fear Him lack nothing"* (Psalm 34:10). By pertaining to the Lord, we become holy, consecrated people, destined to walk in integrity and to serve our God in spirit and truth. By accepting Jesus Christ as our personal Savior and Lord, we have signed a divine contract that states that we are to follow Him in holiness and righteousness all the days of our lives. Attached to this contract were the death certificate of our carnal nature and our new birth certificate.

On the latter, it was mentioned that from now on, we must let ourselves be controlled by the Spirit of God because it is only by His Spirit that it will be possible for us to accomplish the desires of the Lord in us. This contract was contained in a ledger. On this book, there was a label on which one could read: *"Let this book of the law not depart from your mouth; meditate on it day and night, to act faithfully according to all that is written therein; for then you will make your ways prosperous, and then you will have success"* (Joshua 1:8). Here, in a nutshell, is an illustration of what the Lord expects of us when we give our lives to Him and make Him our personal Lord and Savior. Our goal as a child of God should be to maintain a relationship of intimacy with our Lord; that is how our attachment to God will grow. This relationship is crucial because it allows us to know and love our Lord. Love cannot exist without a relationship. You must associate with a person to know him, appreciate him, love him, and be faithful to him.

Beloved in Christ, *"let us know, let us press on to know the Lord"* (Hosea 6:3). Let us have a privileged and personal relationship with Him. May this fellowship with God cause us to renounce earthly desires and lead us to a righteous and happy life. Our titles, possessions, fasting, prayers, or even fewer prophecies will not make us faithful to God. Instead, it is the quality of our relationship with God that will. Only through this process can we succeed and be successful in all respects.

Dear Anonymous,

Your letter itself is the answer to your question. For having written it sufficiently proves that you have an ardent desire to do what is right in the eyes of the Lord. However, no one can choose for you; not even God can choose for you. He shows you the way to go. It's up to you to accept or reject it. Just know that our poor choices can sometimes cause us to miss out on glory (true glory that comes from God, not the one the world gives). You miss all God has prepared for you on earth and in heaven by going your way.

You say that you are attached to your possessions and that it is difficult to give up this life. Do you know that even if you refuse to give up your wealth, you can still lose it? The world quickly forgets and is always looking for new celebrities. What you have today, others have had before you, have it at the same time as you, and will have it after you. However, what never was before you, which is today, will never be after you; it's you. God created you unique on earth and knows you better than anyone. Before you were conceived in your mother's womb, He knew you and destined you for a glorious future, like a star. Indeed, men can discover stars, but they cannot create them. They give names to stars but cannot determine the life span of a star because men die, but the stars remain.

Men raise their heads to observe the stars because they are above them. However, God lowers his head to look at the stars because they are below Him. The stars shine above men, and God shines above the stars. Men magnify the stars, and the stars magnify God, the Creator. The Lord walks on the stars, the stars walk on men, and men walk on grains of sand. Humans manipulate grains of sand, but they don't manipulate stars. Which would you rather be, a star or a grain of sand?

Before answering, I want you to know that all stars, including you, were created by God. Yes, you are a star; like all stars, you must shine. Just as the star of our Lord Jesus Christ was detected, men have also detected your star. They did not create you because only God engenders and makes you shine. The shine He gives to a star remains forever. Before making your choice, ask yourself these questions:

"What is the use of a man gaining the whole world, if it is at the cost of his life? What could he give to redeem his life?" (Mark 8:36-37), *"So, if anyone is ashamed of me and my words in the face of the people of today, who are unfaithful and rebellious to God, then the Son of Man will also be ashamed of him, when he comes in the glory of his Father with the holy angels."* (Mark 8:38)

May the Lord bless you and help you make the right choice.

11

The Power of The Word

"The Word became flesh."
~ John 1:14

Letter from Vanessa

My name is Vanessa, and here is my story: I am a 36-year-old woman, married for thirteen years, and still have no children. My husband and I have tried everything to have a child, from the most natural way to artificial insemination through adoption. We even resorted to a surrogate mother... Yes, we tried everything. We did everything in our power and within our means. I don't even count the number of times I cried out to God, the amount of fasting and prayers I made for the Lord to grant me the grace of having a child.

I listened to and saw the testimonies of other couples in the same situation as me who now have a child today by God's grace. Today, I am discouraged and hopeless. I had so much faith that God would give me the desire of my heart, but because my wish was not granted, I lost faith in God; I don't even believe in miracles anymore. I love the Lord, but deep in my heart, I blame Him for not answering my prayers. However, the word of God tells us: "Ask and it will be given to you." I asked and got nothing. What must I do for God to hear me? I'm at my wit's end, and my frustration is such that I'm angry with everyone. My house is no longer the haven it used to be because I spend my time quarreling with my husband. I blame him for not praying enough for this problem. This situation has separated us from each other, and it has also separated us from the Lord. Please help me. What should I do?

VANESSA.

"In the beginning was the word, and the word was with God. He was with God in the beginning. Through him, all things were made; without him, nothing was made that has been made; In him was life, and that life was the light of all mankind. The light shines over darkness and the darkness has not overcome it" (John 1:3-4). The light was a good thing; God, therefore, sent it to

159

enlighten men because they were in darkness. Thus, to enlighten men, the light became man. Consequently, He made himself like those he wanted to bring out of the darkness. In other words, the word of light has become flesh, therefore human. However, because of His human appearance, the Word was not received by all. Many men did not welcome Him because he looked the same as those, he wanted to bring life to. "Yet *to all who did receive Him, to those who believed in His name, He gave the right to become children of God*" (John 1:12). Those who believed in Him came out of darkness and walked into the light. They could accomplish great things because the Word gave them the power and the capacity to accomplish everything through Him and Him.

In the first chapter of John, this Word of light and life refers to Jesus Christ. The Bible teaches us that He was with God when He created the world, and God made everything through Him. It is, therefore, by the Word that all things exist. Thus, we can obtain everything through the Word because He has creative power. He was made flesh to enlighten us and to allow us to make our words become flesh. Christ became flesh to save us and deliver us from all our chains. He brought us out of our bondage when we walked in darkness. He did not save us to wait for His coming peacefully. He wants us to use Him to illuminate all areas of our lives so that they can be productive. God has given us His word to cause us to bear fruit worthy of repentance. Christ became flesh, and He bore fruit. To follow Him is to produce fruit with the Word given to us.

The Bible said it gave power to all who received Him. The power that allowed us to become children of God is the same that will enable us to receive the desires of our hearts. In the general sense of the term, every word has power. The power to bless and the power to curse. The power to build and the power to destroy. Therefore, it is written that *"The tongue has the power of life and death, and those who love it will eat its fruit"* (Proverbs 18:21). So, we must be cautious about what we put out of our mouths. Unlike our words, the Word of God has only one effect: to give life. Abundant blessings will flow from this life. This life, which is in the Word, will never end. Many of us fail to experience the power of the word of God. Just because we don't have faith in God doesn't mean we can't experience the power of God. Passing from the "word-light" stage to the "word-flesh" stage is difficult.

Following the example of Christ, the Bible teaches us that after having enlightened us, the word must produce fruit, He must become flesh, and we must see this flesh. This is called the works of faith. We start from the invisible word: (the things we do not see) to the word made flesh (the demonstration of the hidden things that have become visible). Thus, if we have not reached the demonstration stage, the word is just a lamp at our feet. We have received and believed in Him; we recognize He has power and is the true light that enlightens all who receive it. However, we don't see the spiritual and physical manifestation of God's word in our life simply because many things prevent that word [1]from being productive in our life. Many things in us stifle this word. Thus, *"we don't let it take root in us, we only cling to it for a moment. And then, when distress or persecution arises because of the word of God, we quickly renounce the faith. Still others... have heard the word, but worldly concerns and the deceptive lure of wealth choke the word, and it produces nothing."* (Matthew 13:21-22)

If we recognize ourselves in this passage, it is a sign that for us, the Word is just a light that illuminates our exterior, not our interior. Now it is precisely in us that the word would like to dwell and act so we can see his works; otherwise, we will speak of faith without works. In other words, we have received the word and recognize that He has power. We are enlightened by Him because those who receive the word are enlightened. Nevertheless, we don't use Him in our day-to-day life or let Him take over all areas of our lives. We know He can change our life completely, but we don't experience His transformative power. For us, the word is simply a lamp at our feet, an excellent way to enlighten ourselves that we use from time to time. Indeed, it is as if you were in a house lit by a lamp, the only source of light it possesses. It would be best if you took this lamp to light you up to go from one room to

---

[1] He or Him are used instead of it when referring to the Word of God, Since Jesus is the word of God.

another. Yet you don't because you think, "What's the point of bothering with a lamp when I know every room in my house by heart?" However, without this lamp, you will walk like a blind person in your house, sometimes bumping into certain obstacles. You will have difficulty finding a lost object in your path because you are moving in complete darkness.

Why move or walk in the dark when we have a lamp to enlighten us? What's the use of having electricity at home if we don't use it and want to stay in the dark? The lamp that we have at our feet is the same one that must lighten our paths. This lighting is not done alone: we must take this lamp and make it the source of light on our way. It is fine to have received the word in our life, but we must not limit ourselves to the stage of reception. We must experience the transformative power of this light. The Lord does not want us to be limited to the stage of receiving His word. We must not just hear, receive, and believe His word. We must, above all, live it and make it alive by testing all its natural and spiritual capacities. He must take complete control of our lives. God sent us the Word, so we live in, for, and through Him. Only in this way will our faith materialize.

The word is not visible; we hear him without seeing him. He is Spirit. It is by faith that we believe in him. So, our faith comes from what we have heard about the Word. As it is written, *"Faith comes by hearing"* (Romans 10:17). If we have listened to something and believed it, we must practice what we have heard and believed to have our testimony of the truthfulness of what has been told to us. Sometimes we ask ourselves why we are not answered when others are; why so and so was they healed of the disease that we have, and we were not; how so and so could have had such an ingenious idea that made him very prosperous. We prayed and tried to apply the same principles, but nothing changed; our situation is still the same. If our situation does not change, it is because we believe in the word of God without being convinced that it can change our life.

Our faith is not active, and this prevents us from receiving our blessings. We must put our faith in the Word. We need to know that it is not *faith* that produces fruit but rather *our faith*. There is a significant difference between faith in its general sense and our faith in the word of God. Our faith in the word of God will cause us to perform as we walk in Christ. Indeed, it is said in Romans 10:17 that *"faith comes by hearing, and hearing by the word of God."* So, it is in vain that we say that we have faith if what we have heard does not come from the word of God or disagrees with what the Word says. Faith should not be born from the testimony of our neighbor but from ours. When we hear, for example, that a person who suffered from the same disease we have was miraculously healed during a prayer crusade, we say to ourselves: "I, too, will go to this crusade to receive my healing. If she were healed, I too would be healed." We go to the crusade with the faith that we will be delivered from this disease. Unfortunately, at the end of the prayer crusade, we return home with the same symptoms of illness. However, there were several miracles, but we did not receive ours. Therefore, we are disappointed and ask the Lord why the others were healed, not us, yet we had faith.

In the above situation, our faith in receiving healing was born from the testimony of a person who suffered from the same disease. We heard what happened in his life. Our faith was born. This is the first step (what we hear). We then went to the same place without being healed. This is the second stage that determines the origin and the level of faith (from whom does what we hear come?). It is this step that will decide whether faith will bear fruit or not. In our example, the faith did not bear fruit simply because it was based not on the word of Christ but on what we had heard about the crusade. If our faith were based on Christ, we wouldn't have to travel to receive our miracle because the Jesus who acted in the campaign is the same one, we received. We have all been given the same power, which works by faith. Only our faith in the word of God counts because it is through it that we are connected to God. In the Epistle of John chapter four, the Bible tells us the story of Jesus Christ and the Samaritan woman. In this story, after talking with the Lord, this woman *returned to the city, where she said to the people: Come and see a man who has told me everything I have done. Could he be the Messiah? So, they left the city and came to find Jesus.* (John 4:28-29)

That day, many Samaritans believed in Jesus Christ through the testimony of this woman who had told them this: *He told me everything that I did* (John 4:39). So, based on this testimony, the Samaritans prayed to the Lord to stay with them. The Lord Jesus Christ, therefore, remained for two days in this city. The Bible tells us that even *more believed because of what He Himself said (John 4:41).* At first, their faith was based on what they had heard from the Samaritan woman. However, when they heard the words of the Messiah for themselves, their faith was no longer based on the woman's testimony but on the word of the Lord. That's why in the end, they had declared to the woman that now *we no longer believe only because of what you told us, but because we have heard Him ourselves, and we know that He is truly the Savior of the world.* (John 4:42)

Our faith should not be based solely on what we hear from the mouths of others. It must also and always be based on the word of God, then on our testimony of what God has done for us. This is very important because not everything comes from the word of God. We live in a world where people have faith in many things. People believe in other gods and other deities. There are even those who only believe in themselves or nothing. In the churches today, some doctrines have nothing to do with the word of God. Teachings that go against the word of God. Nevertheless, because the message comes from the pastor, we believe it without examining it to know if it agrees with the Bible. In Acts 17:10, the Bible tells us that the Jews of the synagogue in Berea had better feelings than the Jews of Thessalonica. *They received the word with great eagerness, and they searched the Scriptures daily to see if what they were told was correct.* (Acts17:11)

We must take the time to study the scriptures like those Jews so that we do not get carried away by every wind of doctrine by receiving teachings that do not come from God. How would we know that a message does not come from God if we do not examine it with the word of God? The Bible contains examples of people who did not believe in our God. Yet He is the one and only true God. Our God is the only one to demonstrate in this world things that we do not see and will never see elsewhere than in His presence and by His power. The prophet Elijah challenged Baal's four hundred and fifty prophets by asking them to offer a bull sacrifice on wood without lighting a fire. He told the people of Israel this: *"They will pray to their god, and I will pray to the Lord. The true God will be the one who answers prayers by kindling the fire"* (1 Kings 18:24). The prophets of Baal invoked their morning god until noon without any response. *Around noon, Elijah began to make fun of them, saying: 'Shout louder!' Since he is a god, he is very busy; or he has an urgent obligation;*

perhaps he is sleeping and needs to be awakened. (1 Kings 18:27)

Despite their cries, they received no response from their god, even though they had shouted very loudly and hurt themselves with swords and spears on purpose. They invoked Baal until the afternoon, but the fire did not light. Then, the prophet Elijah in turn, took a bull and, after having repaired the altar of the Lord, which was in ruins, *"he dug a ditch around the altar that could contain about thirty liters; he arranged logs of wood on the altar, then cut up the bull and placed the pieces on the wood"* 1 Kings 18:32-33). He ordered four pitchers of water to be poured over the sacrifice thrice so that the water flowed all around the altar and even filled the ditch. He then called on the Lord in these terms: *"Lord, God of Abraham, Isaac, and Jacob, show today that you are the God of Israel, that I am your servant, and that it is on your order I did all this. Answer me, Lord, answer me, so that these people know that it is You, Lord, who is the true God"* (1 Kings 18:36). God then sent down a fire which consumed the sacrifice and all that was around namely the wood, the stones, the dust and even the water which was in the ditch was sucked up. When the people saw him, they began to glorify God by saying: *"It is the Lord who is the true God!"*

It was at the command of the Lord that the prophet Elijah caused water to be poured in abundance on the sacrificial altar. Elijah acted by faith in God, and the

Lord demonstrated His power. Baal's prophets also had faith in their god. However, the latter had been unable to lite a fire on dry wood, and his prophets had been killed without his intervention to save them. I do not know what their faith in Baal was based on, but I am sure that the prophet Elijah's faith was based on the word of God.

It is such faith that the Lord asks us to have. Our faith must be commensurate with our God. Our faith should not be based on guesswork but instead on a conviction based on what our Lord declares in His word. Faith is not a behavior but a conviction. In Jesus Christ, anything not done on the principle of faith cannot work. In other words, everything that does not come from faith is a sin (Romans 14:23). This is what the reading of the four Gospels teaches us. When we read the Gospels, we notice that all the people who called on the Lord Jesus were answered, thanks to their faith. Their faith in Jesus healed and delivered them, not Christ's. We are no different from those people who received their miracle from God.

In Jesus Christ, there is no exception to the rule; instead, there is an exception through faith. Our faith makes a difference in how we receive things from the Lord. It is by faith that we are united to Jesus. However, it is only through the demonstration of our faith that Jesus connects with us. We must know we can connect with Jesus without Him being united with us. To believe in God is to be united with Him.

However, when we put our faith in His word by believing that everything He says comes to pass, we are one flesh with Him. We must therefore remain united to the Lord so that He may unite with us. Jesus Himself said, "he who remains united to me, and to whom I am united, bears much fruit" (John 15:7). Chance does not exist with God, even enchantment. Everything we want from the Lord will pass through our faith in His word.

The Lord always said this to those who sought His help:

"Rise and go, your faith has made you well." (Luke 17:19)

"Your faith has healed you." (Luke 18:42)

"You are now healed because of your faith." (Matthew 9:22)

"When Jesus saw their faith, he said to the paralyzed man, your sins are forgiven." (Mark 2:5)

"It shall be done for you as you have believed." (Matthew 8:13)

"Your faith is great; it shall be done for you as you desire." (Matthew 15:28)

"Your faith has healed you, go in peace." (Mark 5:34)

Whatever you ask in faith through prayer, you will receive. (Matthew 21:22)

All these biblical references prove that it will always be done to us according to our faith. It is good to believe that God exists and that Jesus Christ, His only son who died for our sins, is our Savior, but it is not enough for the power of God to manifest itself in our life. Believing in God Almighty does not guarantee anything because even *the demons believe it too, and they tremble* (James 2:19). What guarantees us everything and makes everything possible is our faith in God and Jesus Christ, our Savior. Our faith must be based on the word of God. By our faith, we must be sure of what we hope for and be convinced of the reality of what we do not see.

Our faith must embody any word that God speaks; it must make alive any word of God. The Bible says that we must receive the word of God and believe in it. Only through this process will it come to life in us. In other words, he will become "flesh." The word of God is not just a lamp at our feet; he is that lighted lamp that was at our feet that we took to guide us through life so that no aspect would ever be in darkness again.

It is the Word that connects us to the Lord. If we obey His word, he will become "flesh" and materialize. He will make himself visible so that we can testify of the power of God and that He will be glorified. Indeed, the purpose of the word is to bring into existence things that do not yet exist, causing what we have read in His word, which we have believed, and which is invisible, to become visible, palpable, in a word "flesh." The

Word of God sees what our eyes cannot see and hears what our ears cannot hear. It can be in places that are miles away from us. The Word of God knows no limit. Therefore, it is written that *"everything is possible to him who believes."* (Mark 9:23)

Everything is possible, and nothing is impossible with faith. Men of faith are the true friends of God because only faith pleases God, and we know that *"without faith it is impossible to please God"* (Hebrews 11:6). If we have faith, we have God, and if we have God, then nothing and no one in this world, underground, in the sea and the heavens will be able to resist us. Everything we confess with our mouths will come to pass. In other words, it will become a reality. All who trust him and believe will see his power's manifestation. The word has been given to us so we can succeed through him, regardless of our situations. If we follow God's Word with faith, we will overcome adversity.

As a Christian, knowing that only our faith pleases God is essential. All that interests Him in us is only our faith and nothing else. God will never act in our life out of pity but according to our faith. Some will wonder what it takes to have faith that pleases God. The answer is found in the Bible and our personal relationship with God. Our everyday life must be a life of faith. The actions we take every day should all be acts of faith, whether in secret with God or in public before men. Nothing in our life should be done without our faith in God. Faith is the only thing that attracts the eyes of God

172

to our person. It is through it that God will approve us. Take the example of the heroes of faith.

༺✦༻

We have read that:

By his faith, Abel still speaks even though he is dead. (Hebrews 11:4)

By faith, Enoch was taken to God without having known death. (Hebrews 11:5)

By faith, Noah listened to God's warnings about what was to come that was not yet seen. (Hebrews 11:7)

By faith, Abraham obeyed when God called him. He left without knowing where he was going. By faith, he lived as a stranger in the land God had promised him. By faith, he was enabled to be a father when he was past the age to be one. By faith, he offered Isaac as a sacrifice when God tested him. (Hebrews 11:8-11)

By faith, Joseph, at the end of his life, announced that the Israelites would come out of Egypt. (Hebrews 11:22)

By faith, Moses left Egypt without fearing the king's wrath; he remained firm as if he had seen the invisible God. (Hebrews 11:27)

By faith, the Israelites crossed the Red Sea as if it were dry land. (Hebrews 11:29)

By faith, the walls of Jericho fell after the Israelites

had circled it for seven days. (Hebrews 11:30)

By faith, the servant of a Roman officer was healed by Jesus Christ. The faith of this Roman officer was very great. (Matthew 8:5-13)

By faith, a woman with blood loss for twelve years was healed by touching the hem of Jesus Christ's garment. (Matthew 9:20-22)

By faith, a blind man received his sight. (Luke 18:41-43)

The examples of men and women of faith in the Bible are so numerous that we cannot name them all. In summary, the power of faith is immeasurable. By faith, the weak say they are strong, the barren see their house filled with children, the blind see, the poor become rich, the unbelieving believe, and the abandoned regain self-esteem. Faith makes the impossible possible; obstacles become advantages, dreams come true, and the orphan finds a family. Hope is born during despair through faith, and love springs above hate. We help our enemy; by faith, we forgive all who trespass against us. We resist temptation and accept torture, misery, and trial joyfully, thanks to faith. By faith, we agree to return good for the harm done to us. By faith, the invisible creates the visible.

Can we stop and think for a moment: After reading all these examples, let each of us write down on a piece of paper one thing that we have achieved because of our faith in God. Something that, in everyone's eyes, was not possible. Something only possible by faith.

Here is one of the things I was able to accomplish by faith:

By faith, in November 2008, I flew from Gabon to South Korea, passing through South Africa and China with my son when he did not have a visa for South Korea. This same son that I gave birth to on September 3, 2006, when, clinically, I had been declared sterile. Beloved, if, as a child of God, you do not have a single testimony of something you have obtained from God through your faith, it is time to question your faith, for *"just as the body without the spirit is dead, so faith without deeds is dead."* (James 2:26)

The purpose of the word is to be received, believed, confessed, and made concrete. These are the four different stages of faith. If we do not respect the first three steps, that is to say: receive, believe, and confess, we will never achieve the miracle. For our faith to move mountains, it must follow this principle. If we confess the word without having believed it, we cannot say that we have faith, and this is where the problem for many of us lies because we skip the stages. We go from the reception stage to confession without going through the phase of believing.

The goal is not to hear and speak but to hear, believe in our hearts, and speak. For the word to bear fruit, faith must first be in our hearts before we confess the word. By the heart, we believe; by the mouth, we affirm what we have believed. As the apostle Paul wrote: *the word is near you, in your mouth and your heart* (Romans 10:8). Thus, the word must first be in our heart so that we can believe it, then in our mouth so that we can confess it.

The springs of life come from the heart and the mouth. God Himself is only interested in our hearts because He knows that *"for the mouth speaks what the heart is full of" (Matthew 12:34) and "for with the heart one believes and is justified, and with the mouth, one confesses and is saved" (Romans 10:10).* It is therefore from the connection of these two elements that the type of faith that pleases God is manifested. The word of God must be connected to faith to have effects and bear fruit.

Dear Vanessa,

Your desire to have a child is completely normal. However, this desire must not be more potent than your love for God because if that is the case, you are becoming an obstacle to your prayer. *"You want something, but you cannot get it. So, you get into quarrels and conflicts. You don't get what you want because you don't know how to ask God for it" (James 4:2).* Any request to God must be made by faith and faith begins with obedience.

The Bible tells us that *"We will receive from Him whatever we ask. Because we keep his commandments and do what pleases Him" (1 John 3:22).* Among other things, *"everything you ask for in prayer will be yours, if you have faith." (Mark 11:24).* It is not the many fasts and prayers that will ensure that God hears you but rather your faith and your obedience to God. Know that as a child of God, it is no longer our will but that of the Lord that is done in our life. Your love for God should not be determined by whether God grants you to have a child or not. Humble yourself before the Lord and change your attitude, let Him be the center of your life, and you will see He will bless you beyond what you can think or imagine. Do not doubt in your heart; instead, have the assurance that God hears your prayers. The Bible teaches us that *"we can look to God with boldness because He listens to us if we ask anything according to His will. Knowing therefore that He hears our prayers, we also have the certainty of obtaining what we have asked of Him." (1 John 5:14-15)*

Hannah asked the Lord for a child whom she had promised to dedicate to the Lord in return. The Lord answered her prayer. Hannah became pregnant and gave birth to Samuel because she had consecrated Samuel to the Lord. He *"intervened in favor of*

Hannah: *she again gave birth to three sons and two daughters. As for young Samuel, he was growing up before the Lord."* (1 Samuel 2:21)

Vanessa, I tell you that what God did for Hannah, He can do for you. He has not changed; He remains the same and still acts. If you have faith, you will see the glory of God in your life because *"no one can please God without faith."*

The Bible says, "Whoever approaches God must believe that God exists and that He rewards those who seek Him." (Hebrews 11:6)

Be it unto you according to your faith.

12

God's Plans for Our Life

"For I know the plans I have for you," declares the
Lord, "plans to prosper you and not to harm you,
plans to give you hope and a future."
~ Jeremiah 29:11

Letter from Martha,

*As a Christian, I never thought I would write such a
letter one day. However, I am tired of hiding my
dismay and pain. Why continue to pretend when,
from above, God knows how I feel and what I think
deep in my heart? I feel like my life has no purpose or
meaning. It's as if I just came to this earth to make up
the numbers. I get up every morning to go to a job I
don't like, but I keep the job because I have no choice
since I must pay my bills. Everything I do fails. Even
in my relationships, it's the same thing. Either it's me
who disappoints, or I'm disappointed by the others. I
do not know what to do. Sometimes I even go to
church without much conviction. I go there out of*

habit. I pray and read my Bible occasionally.

This morning, when I got up, I said a prayer where I asked the Lord to tell me why He sent me to this earth. Is there anything specific He wants me to accomplish? I need an answer from Him because I'm losing my taste for life. Does God have a plan for each of His children? If so, how do I know the plan He has for me? I turned 30 today, the age Jesus Christ began His ministry on this earth. I want to follow His example by starting something that values my life, benefits my neighbor, and, above all, agrees with my God.

I want to be what God says I am, not what I think. May God help me by giving meaning to my life. I feel dead, although alive. I've even considered killing myself because I've lost my taste for life. I'm tired of being what I am, meaning nothing at all. I want to be the person God says I am. My questions are: Who am I? Is it still possible to return to the Lord and find my first love for God and my radiance? I feel like I live in darkness. God help me before it's too late.

MARTHA.

In chapter 1 of verse 5 of the book of Jeremiah, God speaks to him in these terms: *"Before I formed you in your mother's womb I knew you, and before you came*

out of her, I had consecrated you, I had established you a prophet of the nations." There is a revelation in this passage that has changed my life since the day I received it. It is a fact that the Lord says that before Jeremiah was conceived in his mother's womb, He already knew him, and before he came out of his mother's womb, He had already been consecrated and established by God as a prophet of the nations. This passage reveals that God consecrates and establishes us for a specific mission before our birth. Thus, no one arrives in this world without the Lord assigning him a precise task to accomplish. He refers to this when He talks about the plans; He has for us. The Lord sends us to this earth with a specific project. He has a unique plan for our life. This plan aims to give us happiness and a future full of hope.

If God says He has consecrated and appointed us for something, it is normal to wonder if we are fulfilling God's plan for our life. As children of God, we must have the conviction of the Lord's call. It is essential to be convinced that what we are doing today, the field of activity we are evolving, is part of God's plan for our life. This conviction is fundamental because *"anything you do against your beliefs is sin"* (Romans 14:23). The term beliefs of which this passage speaks is nothing but faith. We must have a firm assurance of our divine calling on this earth. Everything a born-again Christian does must always be done in faith. We know that without faith, it is impossible to please God. Now, what does not please God is called sin.

The master of sin is the devil. He is the enemy of our soul. He is the one who diverts us from the plans that God has made for us. Many of us have been diverted from the plans for which God intended them. We find ourselves living lives that have nothing to do with our true destiny. The devil's goal is to keep us from doing God's will. Therefore, when he is aware of God's plans for us, he puts strategies to prevent their achievement. Thus, the devil will block what God established as projects of peace. Where the Lord has provided stability, the devil will cause trouble.

God has planned a future and hope for us, but death and despair will occur. Instead of wealth and prosperity, we will have poverty and adversity. Fertility will be replaced by sterility. Instead of health, we will have an illness. Marriages will end in divorce and the premature death of one of the spouses. People will baselessly prefer celibacy to marriage. The body that God had consecrated as the temple of the Holy Spirit will become the residence of demonic spirits sent by the devil to prevent us from enjoying our life. This is how the devil somehow works to stifle God's purposes in our lives. This strategy is not new. When we read the Bible from Genesis to Revelation, we see how the devil repeatedly tries to lead God's children away from their destiny by making them rebellious and disobedient to the word of God. He did that in the Garden of Eden with Adam and Eve.

The Lord created man in His image and likeness, making him an eternal being. Indeed, when he established man in the Garden of Eden, God commanded the man: *"You are free to eat from any tree in the garden, but you must not eat from the fruit of knowledge of good and evil, for when you eat from it, you will certainly die"* (Genesis 2:16-17). This biblical passage proves that if Adam had not eaten the fruit of the knowledge of good and evil, he would have never died. God's plan for man was that he would never know evil and live forever. But the devil, having learned of this plan, decided to ensure it did not come true. So, he tempted the man who succumbed to it to the detriment of his eternity. God thus expelled him from the Garden of Eden, where he lived peacefully, to where he would have *"to work the ground from which he had been taken" (Genesis 3:23).*

What the devil did with Adam and Eve, he continues to do with us today. Many of us have even been tested from our mother's womb, others from their early childhood. Even before we were born, the devil had already prepared a plan to block our destiny. Do you think it's God's plan that people abort, that babies are born struggling between life and death? Or that children die, women miscarry, or die in childbirth? From Genesis to Revelation, there are several stories where men of God encounter obstacles intended to prevent them from accomplishing the will of God. If the Bible says that before we came out of our mother's womb, God had established and consecrated us for a particular task, we must know that before we were born, the devil prepared his plans against us. The story of Moses and our Lord Jesus Christ are two examples that confirm this reality.

◦⊙◦

The example of Moses:

In the first chapter of the book of Exodus, the Bible says that the Pharaoh had given this order to the two Hebrew midwives: *"When you help the Hebrew women to give birth, take a good look at the child that is born: if it is a boy, kill him, if it's a girl, let her live* (Exodus 1:16). Thus, Moses had not even been born when the Pharaoh gave this order to the midwives. The devil knew that God would raise among the people of Israel a man who would free His people from the bondage of the Egyptians. He knew this liberator was not among the present generation of Israel but was to be part of the coming generation. That's why he ordered the killing of all newborn boys because he knew the liberator would be a man, not a woman.

The pharaoh, seeing that the people of Israel were increased abundantly, decided to kill all the little boys so that the population of Israelites would not increase further. The devil inspired Pharaoh to kill Moses, whom God had already established as the deliverer of his people. Nevertheless, the midwives did not obey the pharaoh and did not exterminate all the little boys born in the Hebrews' families. When he realized that the midwives had not followed his order and that the Israelites had become increasingly numerous and very strong, he ordered his people to throw every Hebrew newborn male to the Nile River. Moses was born in this same period and was rescued from the waters of the Nile River by the Pharaoh's daughter. In this way, the enemy's plan to kill Moses failed. Throughout his life, Moses fulfilled the plans the Lord had consecrated him. The Bible says that in Israel and even today, *"There has never again been a prophet in Israel like Moses. The Lord spoke face to face with him and sent him to perform powerful miracles in the presence of the king of Egypt and his entire nation. No one else has ever had the power to do such great things as Moses did for everyone to see.* (Deuteronomy 34:10-12)

The example of Jesus Christ our Lord and Savior:

As with Moses, the devil attempted to frustrate the plan of liberation that God had established for mankind through His only begotten Son, Jesus Christ our Savior. Indeed, when Mary, the mother of Jesus Christ, found herself pregnant by the action of the Holy Spirit, her fiancé Joseph, who did not want to denounce her publicly, had decided to break off her engagement secretly. However, even if Joseph secretly broke off the engagement to protect her, Mary's pregnancy would still have ended up being seen in Nazareth in Galilee. She would have been stoned to death according to Jewish law. The stoning of Mary was the devil's first attempt to prevent Christ's coming into the world. Glory be to God, who sent His angel to Joseph to reassure him about the child Mary was carrying. God revealed to Joseph that it was by the action of the Holy Spirit that his fiancée was pregnant and that he should not be afraid to take her as his wife.

After reassuring Joseph about Mary's pregnancy, the angel informed him about God's plans for this child. The plan was filled with happiness, peace, and hope. Joseph was told by the angel that *"Mary will give birth to a son and that he will call him Jesus because He will save His people from their sins."* (Matthew 1:21)

The devil did not abandon his plan to kill the Lord Jesus Christ. After failing to sever the marriage, he attempted to kill the child at the time of delivery. While Joseph and Mary were in Bethlehem for the census, the day Jesus was born arrived. Unfortunately, there was no place for them in the hotel industry. She brought our Lord into the world in a manger, where cattle are kept. Mary, who was carrying her first child, gave birth in the wrong place without the assistance of a midwife. This could have caused complications during childbirth and led to her or the child's death. This attempt by the devil to prevent the birth of Christ failed once again. However, after this failure, he looked for another way to kill the child after it was born. The Bible tells us, *"When Herod realized that the wise men had deceived him, he was very angry. He gave the order to kill all little boys under the age of two in Bethlehem and the surrounding areas."* (Matthew 2:16)

As we see in this passage, the devil will stop at nothing when he wants to block the fulfillment of God's plan in our lives. Because of only one child, several children were massacred, but glory returned to God, who, by one of His angels, warned Joseph in a dream. He had ordered him to take the child and his mother and flee to Egypt and stay there until God asked him to return. Thus, God always warns His children about the plans He has for them.

As children of God, we must ask Him to reveal to us the plans He has for our children and us. Christians should pray to God: *"Lord, reveal your plans for the child I am carrying. Please tell me in which area you had devoted and established him because you say that before we conceived this child, you already knew him."* This prayer is vital because if we have the revelation of God's plan for our children, we will be better equipped to help them fulfill their destinies.

The Bible says we perish for lack of knowledge. He who knows his call does not allow himself to be diverted from his destiny. He keeps his eyes fixed on his goal; whatever the times and circumstances, he is not discouraged. He trusts in God, who always accomplishes His plans in due time. Joseph and Mary knew the plans God had for Jesus Christ. The angel Gabriel announced to Mary that the child she would give birth to would be great and that he would be called the Son of the Most High God, and that *the Lord God will make him a king like his ancestor David. He will rule over the people of Jacob forever; His kingdom will never end.* (Luke 1:32-33)

God warns them because He does not want his parents to divert his destiny. The upbringing they give him might lead him to do things that are contrary to what God has planned. We all know this verse from Proverbs 22:6 which asks us to *instruct the child according to the way he must follow, and when he grows up, he will not turn away from it.* In this passage, the Bible says that the child must be brought up according to *the way he must follow.* The way mentioned in the word of God in this passage refers to the plans the Lord has for the child, as He said in the book of Jeremiah 29:11. It is on the path of His plans that we must guide our children and even ourselves if we find ourselves on a way contrary to the one the Lord would have us take.

The Christian life is not a life of chance or surprises. God never allows himself to be surprised and never surprises His children. All who have an authentic relationship with Him know the Lord's promises to them in advance. When asked, God always tells us what He expects of us on this earth. He reveals His plans to us and gives us the direction He would have us take so that we are in His perfect plan. The word of God declares that even if the prophecy takes time to be fulfilled, we must be patient and wait because it will undoubtedly be fulfilled. The adverb certainly is used here to qualify a thing that is indubitable, and of which one is convinced of the realization. When the word of

God tells us to wait for the fulfillment of God's promises, He means to tell us that we should not be discouraged or turn away but trust that what God says will surely come to pass. Our only role is to stand firm by holding on to the word and keeping our eyes fixed on God. However, to stand firm, we must know God's plans because the devil will do everything to prevent us from entering God's perfect plan.

One who does not know God's plans for his life cannot protect himself against the enemy's attacks. It is impossible to preserve a treasure of which one does not know its existence. We are important in the eyes of God. He knows exactly what we need, and only from Him can we get the best for our life. This best is found in the plans or promises He has made to us. He has a plan for us and knows how to accomplish it better than anyone. This plan existed even before we were born and even before our parents were conceived. God knows us better than ourselves and what is good for each of His children. Therefore, as children of God, we must not limit ourselves to confiding our plans to Him but also strive to know whether these plans are part of the plans He had intended for us.

Before our new birth in Jesus Christ, we walked according to our understanding and were guided by our flesh, not the Holy Spirit. Now that we are a new creature, we must live by the One in whom we have believed. He drew us to Himself to do His will. And that will begin by asking Him to show us His plan and guide us on the right path. Let's not be satisfied with what we already have because perhaps the Lord has planned greater things than now. Understand that these things will never manifest unless we ask the Lord for them and work for them. Let us not forget that *the Kingdom of heaven has suffered violence, the violent take it by force* (Matthew 11:12). Our priority as Christians is to *seek first the Kingdom and righteousness of God* (Matthew 6:33). Now, the only way to obtain the Kingdom of God is to do His will, and God's will be to accomplish His perfect plan for our lives. Thus, God sends us to earth with a specific project. This plan is His will for our life.

Even the Lord Jesus Christ our Savior, one day while speaking to His disciples, told them this: *I came down from heaven not to do my will, but the will of Him who sent me. And this is what the One who sent me wants: that I do not lose any of those whom He entrusted me with, but that I raise them from death on the last day. Yes, this is what my Father wants: that all who see the Son and believe in Him have eternal life and that I raise them from death on the last day.* (John 6:38-40)

The Lord Jesus reveals in this passage the reason for which He was sent to earth, in a word, the will of God for His life. Today we are saved, and we can inherit eternal life because Jesus Christ fulfilled his mission and continues to do so to this day so that many are saved. God's plans for us always end up being accomplished when we allow ourselves to be led by

Him. Whatever the duration, times, and circumstances, His plans always come to pass when we are faithful to Him and let Him take control of our lives. If there is one thing we should desire as Christians, it is God's plan for our lives because this plan is the mark we will leave on earth. The work produced by this mark will always bear fruit and, at the same time, bring joy to the heart of God. We must ask the Holy Spirit to reveal to us the plans of God; the Bible says that the Holy Spirit certifies the desires of God in us. Only through Him can we have the revelation of God's plans for us. The Holy Spirit's role is to connect us with God. Indeed, *the Spirit can examine everything, even the most deeply hidden plans of God.*

In the case of a man, only his own mind knows the thoughts within him; likewise, only the Spirit of God knows the thoughts of God. We have not received the spirit of this world; but we have received the Spirit that comes from God, so that we know the gifts that God has given us (1 Corinthians 2:10-12). So, nothing we do in Christ should be done without the guidance of the Holy Spirit because God is Spirit. Any connection with Him must be with His Spirit. Besides, isn't it written that God *is Spirit and those who worship Him must worship Him in spirit and in truth* (John 4:24). It is only through His Spirit within us that we can connect with Him to know the plans He has for us. Let no one say that he asked God to let him know his plans but got no response.

The Lord always answers this prayer because He knows that this prayer is decisive for our destiny, and He does not want us to deviate from His plans. However, this happens when we allow ourselves to be guided by our intelligence and strength, by the flesh. It is good to walk in harmony with God on the path He has traced for our life under the direction of His Spirit because it is only on this path that we will be happy and at peace. This happiness and peace will come from knowing that we have accomplished the mission for which God brought us to this earth. It is in the fulfillment of this mission that our prosperity lies. I'm talking about prosperity that goes beyond material possessions. This state of mind allows us to be happy and at peace with God whether we are rich, poor, sick, healthy, married, or single, with children or not. Our hearts are not troubled when we know we are walking in harmony with God.

The Spirit of God and ours are in tune. This relationship with God is essential to accomplish His projects for us and experiencing true happiness. However, knowing that God has a plan for us is good; wanting to fulfill that plan is pure desire. However, we must know Him to accomplish this plan because we cannot concentrate on something unknown.

Hence the following question:

How do we know what plans God has for us?

Indeed, each of us has a goal to accomplish that has been set by God. The Lord wants us to discover this purpose and fulfill it. It is to achieve this purpose that we have come to this earth, and it is only through this plan that we will see the manifestation of the glory of God in our lives. Success in the eyes of the Lord is characterized by accomplishing the projects He has formed for us. So, to know God's plan for our life, we must meditate on his word. It is in it that the secrets of life are found.

The advice He gave to Joshua in the past is the same as He gives us today: Do not let *this book of the law depart from your mouth, meditate on it day and night, to act faithfully according to everything that is written there; for it is then that you will be successful in your undertakings, it is then that you will succeed* (Joshua 1:8). It is by meditating on His word and praying to God that the latter will reveal His projects to us, and it is also by relying on His word that we will be able to carry out our projects and that they will succeed. The word of God is the only and the true way to know His plans. It's all in His word. By meditating on the word, we will find good advice in the face of life situations.

The word of God is *a lamp to our feet, a light on our way* (Psalm 119:105). Therefore, to know His will, let us meditate on His word and keep sight of the guidance therein. Let us keep them in our hearts and put them into practice because they will bring life to those who welcome them. By observing God's word and conforming to His precepts, we will have the revelation of His plans and that these plans can be accomplished. Once we know God's plans, we must obey Him. It may happen at first sight that His plans do not please us or that they seem impossible to our eyes. Even if that's the case, let's just be obedient, and we'll see that in the end, the Lord's will is always what's best for us. The Lord will never lead us down a path that can harm us.

You know, God's plan already existed before we were conceived. This specific plan was waiting for the right person to carry it out. God, who knows everything and is the Creator of everything, has seen us as the right person to accomplish this project. This is no accident or coincidence. We are the right person in the right place for the right project. God never makes mistakes. This mission that the Holy Spirit has revealed to us through the Word is ours, and we have no excuses for not accomplishing it.

We must arm ourselves with courage and strength to do the will of the Lord. We should never forget that we are not alone, the Lord is with us, and He will never abandon us. That's the same thing He said to Joshua, *"I'll never forsake you, never leave you helpless." Be brave and strong...it will be enough for you to be courageous and strong and keep the law fully"* (Joshua 1:6-7). What was valid in the past for Joshua is also valid for us today. God has not changed, and even His word. As it is written, *"Heaven and earth will pass away, but my words will not pass away"* (Matthew 24:35). If His words remain the same, then why not seek in them the purpose of our life and our happiness, like those who have gone before us?

Unlike our predecessors, we have the Holy Spirit as our permanent guide in addition to the Word. The Lord sent him to lead us into all truth. The Holy Spirit knows all the plans God has for us. If God knew us before we were in our mother's womb, the Holy Spirit, who is nothing other than the Spirit of God, also knew us before we came to earth because He and God are one. The Lord hides nothing from His Spirit. Thus, it is by Him and through Him that the Lord will reveal the plans He has for us. The Holy Spirit is the best guide for carrying out God's will. Jesus Christ said the Holy Spirit *"shall not speak of Himself, but He will speak whatever He hears, and He will tell you things to come."* (John 16:13)

There are things that the Holy Spirit has heard the Lord say about us that concern our destiny and that He wants to announce to us so that we can accomplish them. He was with God at the beginning when Earth and Heaven were created. He also was with God when we were created. Nothing that concerns us is unknown to Him; therefore, our Lord Jesus Christ sent Him to us so that through Him He might announce to us great things, hidden things, which we do not know, as written in Jeremiah 33:3. Thus, with the word of God and the Holy Spirit we have the necessary equipment to know and accomplish the plan of God. Therefore, the revelation of our destiny is found in meditation of the word, prayer, obedience, faithfulness, and faith in God. We must trust in the Lord and seek to always do His will in everything we do or want to do. Everything we do must be consistent with God's plan for our lives.

The advantage of knowing God's plans is that it allows us to be focused and prevents us from getting lost or wasting our time on projects that are not ours. When we know and walk according to God's plan, we have confidence because we know where we are going, and our eyes remain fixed on our objective. We know we are on the right path and in the company of the right guide. So, we have no fear. In Psalm 32:8, the Lord speaks to us in these terms: *I will teach you and show you the path you should take, I will be your adviser, my eyes will watch over you.* Isn't it wonderful to see how God does everything so we don't miss our life's purpose? He wants to be our counselor to direct us throughout our lives.

Sometimes we go far to seek the solution to our problems when it is right by our side. Life and happiness are in the word of God, and all who rely on it will never be disappointed. The devil knows it. Therefore, he does everything to prevent us from meditating and obeying the word of God. He knows that if he succeeds in leading us away from the word of

God, we will never be able to accomplish the plans God has made for us. The devil knows that each person God sends to Earth is a star that must shine in a specific area. Therefore, when it detects a star, it puts strategies to steal it, so it does not shine.

The galaxy has approximately two hundred and four hundred billion stars. Yet despite this infinite number of stars in the sky, the three Wise Men could detect the star of Christ. They noticed something different in it compared to the other stars. That's why they asked: *where is the child who has just been born, the king of the Jews? We saw his star when it rose and have come to worship him* (Matthew 2:2). If the Wise Men could see the star of our Lord, they who were exact as us, do not think that our star would be hidden. The Lord Jesus clarified that you *don't light a lamp and put it under a bushel, but on a stand, and it gives life to all in the house. Thus {our} light must shine before men, that they may see the good that {we do} and praise {our} Father which is in heaven.* (Matthew 5:15-16)

As this passage says, the role of all light is to illuminate, and everything that shines attracts attention. Therefore, because of our brilliance, the enemy attacks us. He can't blame those with no shine because they already belong to him. The opposite of light is darkness. He is the master of darkness and aims to extinguish our light. It can only achieve its purpose if we stray from the word of God. The Word is a powerful weapon to resist the adversary and to stand firm. The

Bible says that the word of God is a sword given by the Holy Spirit. This word is *living and active, sharper than any two-edged sword* (Hebrews 4:12). It is the offensive weapon that the Christian must use to keep burning the flame that God has put in him to triumph over the world.

We now know how to fulfill God's plan for our lives. Let's save time on projects that are not ours. God's plans are the best, so we must focus on seeking the Lord's will rather than on our desires. It is crucial to follow His will, even contrary to our wishes, because we will gain a lot by doing what the Lord expects of us. Only in His plan will we find true fulfillment. Even when it is difficult to achieve, God's plan always gives us happiness.

In Gethsemane, the Lord Jesus felt sadness and anguish before His arrest. He addressed His disciples in these terms: *My soul is overwhelmed with sorrow to the point of death* (Matthew 26:38). Thus, the will of God can be painful and even shocking in some cases. It can be challenging to obey him. Even Jesus Christ, our Savior and Lord asked God *to remove this cup of pain from Him if possible.* Even for Him, the only begotten Son of God, it was painful. However, He added: "My Father, if it is not possible for this cup to be taken away unless I take it, may your will be done" (Matthew 26:42). He preferred to do the will of God rather than give in to fear and renounce God's plan.

This cup was hard to drink, but He drank it and endured all kinds of suffering and humiliation, but it was the price to pay for us to be saved. Because of what He endured, His name is above all names, and He alone is "worthy *to receive power, wealth, wisdom, strength, honor, glory, and praise*" (Revelation 5:12). God's plan was for Jesus Christ to save us from all our sins, and He did. By accomplishing this project, He has made His Kingdom eternal. All those who, like Jesus Christ, agree to fulfill God's plan for their life by relying on His word will change the lives of the greatest number by carrying out God's plan for their life and, after that, inherit eternal life. It is eternal life that God is referring to in Jeremiah 29:11 when He speaks of giving us a future and hope. This hope is nothing other than the inheriting of eternal life: the reward of all who overcome the world through their union with Jesus Christ and obedience to His word.

As with Jesus Christ, even though God's plan for our lives includes painful trials, we must not back down in the face of this adversity. Let's trust the Lord. If He gave us this project, it is because He knows that we can accomplish it. The Lord is faithful; He will never form a project beyond our strength, whatever the trials of the moment. Let's not lose heart because God is not done with us yet. He is the One who creates a path even when everything seems closed. This path already existed. It's just that we've been pushing off that path by our rebellion. It may also turn out that this rocky path we are on now is the one God has laid out for us to accomplish His plan in our lives. If this is the case, let's take courage and trust in the Lord because He will never abandon us.

He wants us to know that *"His thoughts are not our thoughts, and our ways are not His ways. As the heavens are high above the earth, so are His ways above our ways, and His thoughts above our thoughts* (Isaiah 55:8-9). It is our attitude to the test that will determine our success. We will never know what God has in store for us until we achieve the goals, He has set for us. We get a glimpse of God's mind because His ways are unfathomable. We must complete the work He asks us to do as Christ our Lord completed His to know the fullness of His mind and enjoy all our blessings. God has made everything available so we can lead a life that glorifies Him and that we are happy on this earth. He never changes His plans and sends us to the world with a plan B. God gives us one plan to accomplish, not two.

From this project, we will draw our blessings, which will be the reward for our work. So out of any situation, He can open a way. No matter how we start, if we are faithful to God, stay in His ways, and work tirelessly, He will prosper us in every way. Always remember that *the end of a thing is* better than its beginning (Ecclesiastes 7:8). With God, we always end up with a happy ending that makes us forget all the suffering and trials we have undergone along the way to fulfilling His plan. All men to whom God has revealed His plan for their lives have had happy endings, despite persecutions and trials. From Abraham to Jesus Christ via Jacob, Joseph, Moses, Joshua, David, Job, Daniel, and many others whom the Bible calls the heroes of faith, all had a happy ending through their obedience to God. So let us consider the end of their life and be their imitators.

Dear Martha,

God wants *"everything to go well with you and to be as healthy physically as you are spiritually (3 John 1:2)*. This is the Lord's desire for you. The Lord's plans for you are beyond what you can think or imagine. They are projects of happiness and not of misfortune to give you a future and hope. However, you must get closer to Him to see these projects come true in your life. Call on God, and He will answer you. Seek spiritual health because he who strays from God is considered spiritually ill. But if spiritually we are sick, we are considered dead, even if physically we are healthy.

Martha, are you in good spiritual health? This is the first question you must ask yourself because the answer to this question will allow you to situate yourself in your relationship with God. By reading your letter, I can already answer this question. Therefore, knowing that you are not in good spiritual health, I recommend that you follow this treatment developed by the best of doctors, who is none other than our Lord and Savior,

Jesus Christ.

Listen to His words for you: "Martha, *my beloved, there is still time now to come back to me, but do it with all your heart: fast, weep, and beg me. It's not enough to lament; it's your heart that needs to be changed. Yes, come back to me, your God: I am benevolent and compassionate, patient and immensely kind, always ready to renounce my threats... And shower you with blessings (Joel 2:12-14). Why ask me who you are in my eyes? Did I not tell you that "you are the salt of the earth and the light of the world?" (Matthew 5:13-14)*

The purpose of the light, in fact, is to shine in order to illuminate all that is dark within you and around you. Therefore, you must ensure that this light never goes out. If its glow wanes like the five wise virgins, always have oil on hand to keep the flame going so it never goes out. This oil you need is the word of truth, which is the light of life. Know that only light activates the light. To maintain your flame, you must be constantly connected to a light greater than yours. Jesus Christ is that light because He is the light of the world.

Light attracts light, and darkness recoils before light because it lays bare all their works. Martha, never forget that Jesus Christ, your Savior, is the light of the world. *"He who follows will have the light of life and will never walk in darkness again" (John 8:12).* So, get up from where you fell and reconnect to the source of life, and you can find the first love you had because He *"keeps the memory of what you once were, as you were to me tied up when you were young" (Jeremiah 2:2). "I know that you love me and care for me. Therefore, be faithful unto death, and I will give you the crown of victory, eternal life. (Revelation 2:10)*

May the Lord our God restore you.

13

The Escape

"Run for your life, don't look back; don't linger in the area; take refuge in the mountains if you want to stay alive."
~ Genesis 19:17

We have been taught many subjects since our conversion: faith, prayer, grace, faithfulness, the power of the Holy Spirit, perseverance... the list is very long. So many teachings on various subjects, each more uplifting than the next, strengthen us in our walk with God.

Are you like me, who has never received a single teaching on fleeing since I became a Christian? I asked myself several times whether it was normal for a child of God to choose to escape in the face of adversity. I asked myself this question at a time when the only solution I had to get out of it was to flee. I will be honest with you and tell you the truth.

I am still going through that period of my life up to now. Even as I write this book, I am going through great adversity in my home. I did everything to overcome it, but it is stronger than me. It's been going on for five years, going from bad to worse. This man so beat me that I sometimes lost my memory for several days. I have endured this for five years. One night he tried to strangle me in my sleep. All this is nothing compared to what I have just discovered. I don't even have the strength to talk about it.

Ana's inexpressible sighs

- Lord, help me! It's stronger than me. You say you don't test us beyond our strength. What I have in front of me is beyond my strength. I endured everything, even the worst humiliations, like taking his mistress to our apartment and having sex on our marital bed or the time he went to spend the weekend in a city with our son and one of his mistresses: my son was only four years old. When they returned, my son asked me why his father slept on the same bed as his new aunt as he slept with me. I didn't know what to tell him; I was so shocked. When I confronted him about this story, the only response I could get was a punch in the face and several kicks to the stomach.

One day he struck me that I lost sight for an hour and

a half. If it was just the beatings, maybe I could still take it. Unfortunately, he always said negative words about me and did it before our son. I do not have any more strength. I feel weak. I must do something about it.

- Lord, you are the One who opens a way when everything seems closed. Father, have mercy on me, I beg you. It's too much for me; I have just lost my mother. My son is only six years old. He still needs me. I have only You in this foreign country. You are my only recourse. Who else could I turn to? It is only from You that my help will come.

I'm so weak that if he raises his hand on me again, I don't think I'll be able to get out of this. He told me it was his house and had the right to do whatever he wanted. Is that true, my God? Does he have the right to spend the weekend with his mistress in our apartment while I'm away?

I do not understand anything anymore. Someone explains to me if it's not normal for me to complain and if it's normal for him to start beating me in front of our son. What have I done to deserve such punishment? People will judge me if I decide to leave, but can they take what I put up with?

Now, as if that wasn't enough, I see videos of him making love to another woman.

- Lord, tell me what to do. From the bottom of my heart, I cry out to You because I am desperate. It hurts. I have no home. My home is in You, Father. Now take control of this situation. I can't do anything on my own. I'll wait on you. I wonder if I will finish this book I'm writing.

Yesterday he threatened to break into my computer and destroy my USB key. I got down on my knees, cried, and begged him not to do so. I left the matrimonial bedroom. I sleep on the floor on a blanket in my son's room. I no longer feel safe with this man. I must get up several times a night to check that my son's door is locked.

Tonight, he wanted to lay his hand on me again when I was barely out of the emergency room. My son called the police, and they called the ambulance because they found me unconscious in my room. He told me I was free to leave if I wanted to but that if I left, the child would stay with him. I don't want to abandon my child. I can't leave him. If my life depends on him, then I will lose my life. I was the same age as him when my mother left me with my brothers and sisters at my father's house. I refuse to let history repeat itself.

How do I go with him? He will never let me go with the child, and he knows I care very much about this child. I'm in so much pain that I can't breathe well. I am writing this book with tears in my eyes because I don't know if this book will ever be published.

- I trust in You, Lord, answer my prayer. Please tell me what I should do. I'll wait for you. I am nothing without you. The little of me that I have left is in You. I expect Your response. I will do as You wish. The path You will ask me to take to get out of my misfortune is the one I will take.

I have decided to fast and pray from tomorrow and sleep on the ground until You speak to me to get me out of this hell. I will not rest my soul, body, and spirit until You tell me what to do. My life is in danger, and my faith is being tested. I have only two alternatives: stay and die or leave and live. But how to leave, knowing that I left my only child behind? Is there a way to go with him? If yes, what is this method? He will never let me go with his child. Speak to me, Lord; I need an answer from You.

As I write this book, I am more and more challenged. Writing this book is a challenge. I am walking toward God's plan for my life. The further I go, the darker the path in front of me becomes. It's like I'm slowly dying. I draw my energy from my faith in God. When I look at my life, the one thing I'm proud of is that I never lost my faith. My faith is my rock. I know You will do anything for me. When I look at myself in the mirror, I ignore my physical appearance; I go beyond the physical eyes and look at myself with the eyes of faith.

The reflection that the mirror gives me tells me that I

must change something. It returns the image of a person whom God has not abandoned. It is the image of a person who needs God's help to transform her life. The first step to becoming that person is to flee.

- Lord, confirm to me that this solution comes from You. Lord, is this really what You want me to do?

At first, I was confused, but as that word echoed in my mind, I came to believe it was a call from the Lord. God's answer to my prayer was to flee. Why would God ask me to run when He could change my husband's heart and transform our home? I still had hope, despite all the suffering I was going through, that things could change because nothing was impossible with God. It is He who touches and changes the heart of man. What was the Lord trying to get me to understand? What exactly does the word escape mean? Why? Under what conditions does a person have to flee? What is the difference between giving up and running away? Finally, most importantly, under what circumstances does God ask a person to flee?

The Bible has several examples of men and women God asked to run. What happened to them after they fled? As a child of God, it is important to always refer to the Bible in everything we do. The Bible is the book of examples par excellence, regardless of our problem.

This is how pushed by the Holy Spirit, I opened my Bible and began to meditate on the term escape, and it was only after this meditation that I understood that, indeed, the Lord wanted me to run away. Escaping is, indeed, different from abandonment. To abandon, according to the dictionary, means to leave something definitively, to no longer pursue something that was in progress or planned. In contrast, fleeing is defined as the act of quickly leaving a place to escape a threat, a real or supposed danger. Thus, a person only flees when his life is in danger.

My life was in danger, and my only alternative was to flee. So, I had to obey the Lord by running away; at this point, it became a matter of life or death. When the Lord asks us to flee, we must obey. God will not ask us to do anything that is not for our benefit. He is our Father, and He knows better than anyone what is good for us. When He asks one of His children to flee, He has already seen that if we stay in this place, we will die, or something terrible may happen. Also, because He loves us and knows the limit of our strength, He knows what we can withstand. He does not want that, when faced with a situation or trial, to be at the end of our strength.

We are tempted to do something that will disqualify us in His eyes. "The *temptations that we have known have all been those that normally come to men. God is faithful to His promises, and He will not allow us to be tempted beyond our strength*" (1 Corinthians 10:13).

So, the only time God asks us to run away is when He realizes that running away is the only way out. Indeed, there are situations where the only solution is to run away. Sometimes running away is better than suffering, especially when suffering can result in our spiritual death (distancing us from God) or physical death (loss of our life). Dropping everything and fleeing is the option when going through a trial, and we have tried to make things work. Still, the situation remains the same despite all our efforts and supplications to God; on top of that, we feel weaker and weaker.

From Genesis to Revelation, we have many examples of men and women of God who fled to save their lives or to keep their integrity in the eyes of the Lord. Joseph fled from the wife of his master Potiphar so as not to commit an abominable act and sin against God. Sarah *"mistreated Hagar so much that she fled into the wilderness"* (Genesis 16:6). Hagar preferred staying in the desert to suffering under her mistress, Sarah. Jacob ran away from Laban because he changed his attitude towards him when he realized Jacob was getting tremendously rich. The Bible tells us in 1 Samuel 27: 1 that "David *said in his heart, "I shall now perish one day by the hand of Saul. There is nothing better for me except that I escape into the land of the Philistines."*

King David had this thought when God already chose him to be the new king of Israel. However, this did not stop him from fleeing King Saul's attacks. David knew that if he didn't run away, Saul would kill him. He could, therefore, no longer stay next to Saul because the latter wanted him dead. David had all the evidence in front of him. King Saul made his intention to kill David known to his son Jonathan. One day, he even threw his spear at David, but the latter dodged it, and the spear stuck in the wall.

After this episode, David fled to the country of the Philistines. If you are in a situation that puts your life in danger and constantly causes you to live in fear of death, you must flee. Many people have died simply because they refused to run when they saw the danger coming. They thought they would eventually get through it, but they ended up dying. Escaping is a divine principle; it has nothing to do with a lack of faith or courage. It is simply a matter of seeing danger and deciding to take refuge, to go to a place where this danger cannot reach us.

God does not wish our death; this is the reason why in the face of danger, He can ask us to flee. We will neither be the first nor the last to escape. In Genesis 19, verse 17, the Bible says that the angels asked Lot to flee to the mountain. In the book of Exodus, it is written that *"Moses fled and took refuge in the land of Midian"* (Exodus 2:15). The prophet Elijah *"became afraid and fled for his life."* (1 Kings 19:3)

The beginning of the New Testament tells us that when the Lord Jesus was a child, King Herod sought to kill Him. After the departure of the Wise Men, an angel of the Lord appeared to Joseph in a dream and said to him: "Get *up! Hurry and take with you the child and his mother to Egypt; stay there until I tell you to come back"* (Matthew 2:13). God knew that this child's life was in danger in Bethlehem. *"When Herod realized that the Wise Men had deceived him, he flew into a great rage. He gave orders to kill all boys under two years old in and around Bethlehem."* (Matthew 2:17)

This example shows us that even our God takes no risks when it comes to protecting us. This child of whom this biblical passage speaks to us is none other than our Savior and Lord Jesus Christ. God, who knows the thoughts of our hearts, knew that if Herod did not have specific information about the whereabouts of the Messiah, he would order the killing of all little boys under the age of two. Therefore, he asked Joseph to flee to Egypt to prevent the Messiah from being killed. I know that many people will find it difficult to escape because of the exploits and miracles that the Lord has worked in their lives in the past.

It is normal to think that if God got us out of such a situation in the past, why wouldn't He do it again today? Yes, the Bible tells us that God is the same yesterday, today, and forever. God does not change, it is true, but circumstances change, and who better than the Lord knows what is best for us? Let's not try to be stubborn because of the wonders of the past. The circumstances are not the same.

This is what the story of the prophet Elijah teaches us. The escape of the prophet Elijah may, at first glance, seem inconceivable since he fled because (Jezebel, King Ahab's wife) threatened him with death. She had already slain four hundred and fifty prophets of Baal. God had just manifested His power by showing the Israelites that He is the only true God, and that the prophet Elijah was His servant. Yet that did not stop the prophet Elijah from fleeing when Jezebel threatened to kill him. The prophet Elijah knew Jezebel would eventually kill him to avenge her prophets. The prophet Elijah could decide not to run and tell himself he had no reason to be afraid because God would protect him from Jezebel, as He had done from her prophets. God was able to protect him, but because he was wise, he ran out of danger, and the Lord took care of him in the desert.

The story of the Prophet Elijah shows us that it was God's will for the Prophet Elijah to seek refuge in the desert. Even when he was discouraged and asked the Lord to take his life, the Lord did not listen to his prayer; on the contrary, he sent an angel to bring him food and drink to give him enough strength to walk for forty days and forty nights to Horeb, the mountain of God. So even while we are on the run, the Lord is with us. The Bible says God will never leave us but will always be with us. He will direct our steps and take care of us. It is true that when we escape, we may be afraid at some point or worried because we have left the comfort of our home and church behind. We have left our friends, family, and work. All those people and things we cared about so much.

Running away requires many sacrifices, and it can be painful at first because the future is always uncertain. Therefore, we must never forget that we are not alone because the Lord will be with us during and after the escape. He will only ask us to do something if He gives us the strength and ability to do it. The Bible tells us that when the people of Israel came out of Egypt, *"the Lord went before them by day in a pillar of cloud to guide them along the way and by night in a pillar of fire to give them light; the Israelites could thus walk day and night. The pillar of cloud by day and the pillar of fire by night never ceased to precede them."* (Exodus 13:20-22)

Just as He preceded the people of Israel through the pillars of cloud and fire, He will also precede us when we escape. Today, these pillars are nothing but the presence of the Holy Spirit in our lives. He is the one who reveals the desires of God. He is the perfect guide. God wants to protect us and save our lives from misfortune, so when faced with danger, if he asks us to flee, we must obey him. The Bible says that God does not test us beyond our strength. Therefore, it is better to escape than to fall into temptation. It is better to flee than to die. Yes, running away is better than falling and losing faith.

Running away will undoubtedly lead us to a desert in a moment of loneliness. We will lose many of our loved ones, and some will judge us without knowing what we face. Everyone will want to give their opinion on us and condemn us without even trying to find out why we left. Even when they learn what happened, they will continue to judge you, saying there was no need to flee and that you could have worked things out. All these comments will be useless. If they did nothing while we were persecuted, they would not have an impact after we were gone. Besides, our life belongs to only two people: God and ourselves.

God sees beyond what we can think or imagine; He searches the depths of man's heart. Before we even open our mouths, He already knows what we will say. Nothing is hidden from the eyes of God, and nothing escapes Him. He is the best adviser a man can have in his life. He sees and knows our pain; it is to Him that we cry out to when we are in pain, humiliation, and fear. In God's eyes, our life has the most value. We must first give an account of our life to Him because as a child of God, our life belongs entirely to Him. Therefore, it must be done when He asks us to flee because if we refuse to run when we are in danger, we jeopardize our life and God's plans.

When will you fulfill God's plan for your life if you're still hurting by trying to save a marriage? If your husband spends his time beating you, humiliating you, and telling anyone who would listen that he is going to divorce you, how will you accomplish God's plan with a husband who openly appears in front of his own family with another wife, who justifies his infidelity and who is a Christian, on top of everything? How will you accomplish God's plan if your husband is a drug addict and alcoholic who beats you and your children every time he comes home? How many times have you been to the hospital for domestic violence? How many times have the police come to your house? How many times has he threatened you to death or even tried to kill you to the point that you live in fear? How often have you told yourself this is the last time you will touch this life-ruining drug? But you keep doing it anyway because you want to act like your friends and be accepted in the group.

Let's talk about those who have entered secret societies, where the members indulge in all kinds of abominations and sacrifices for the sole purpose of maintaining social position or gaining success in the eyes of the world: you refuse to renounce these practices because you fear losing your privileges and being judged by men. You didn't have the courage each time you wanted to run away. Deep inside you, you hear the call of the Lord who says to you: Flee these things and *seek righteousness, attachment to God, faith, love, patience, and gentleness. Fight the good fight of faith, pursue eternal life.* (1 Timothy 6:11-12)

Do not harden your heart if you hear this call from the Lord. Many people want to save their marriage, position, relationship, image, and job so badly that they don't even realize they have lost eternal life in their fight and struggle. This brings us back to this question of our Lord Jesus Christ: *"What does it profit a man to gain the whole world if it is at the cost of his life?"* (Mark 8:36)

What can be more important to a human being than his own life? Social status is not worth eternal life. Nothing has more value in our life than the latter. Indeed, inheriting eternal life is the greatest reward we can receive. We cannot risk losing this legacy to anyone or anything. If we must flee to keep this heritage, let us run and not look back. Know that whatever we have had in the past, whatever we leave behind, with God, the best is always yet to come. The Bible says that God will never leave us but will always be with us. Even while we are on the run, the Lord is with us. It is He who will direct our steps and take care of us. Let's not worry about "what people will say." Let us instead concern ourselves with what the Lord thinks of us and our present life. He is the one that holds our life in His hands, and not a human being, not even ourselves. Let us always remember the reason we fled: to save our lives.

We do not run to get lost but to seek the peace, security, and justice of God. So *let us be brave and strong, do not tremble in fear before them, for the Lord our God will walk with us, never forsaking us* (Deuteronomy 31:6). Thus, during our escape, not only will the Lord be with us, but even better, He will lead our steps and take care of us. It may happen that during our escape, we are troubled, afraid, or worried because of what we will leave behind: our everyday life, our comfort zone (a semblance of comfort because there is no comfort in bondage and the absence of peace).

Running away undoubtedly requires courage, involves certain sacrifices, and can be very painful and dangerous. However, we must refuse to cling to things or people that keep us from experiencing happiness and from our blessings. Not everyone is born in Canaan, a land with milk and honey. Some people must cross the desert and all that entails to get there. Many must fight and work hard, distance themselves from certain people, cut off contact with others, and shun specific backgrounds to experience true happiness and receive God's blessing.

Escaping will sometimes lead us to the desert, to a moment of solitude, to a place where we will only hear two voices: ours and that of the Holy Spirit. There will be times of confusion, regret, uncertainty, and discouragement. Even if it happens to us, do not look back and always remember why we are running away: to save our lives and accomplish the thing for which the

Lord sent us on earth.

There is no destiny in a comfort zone. It's time to take charge of our lives and decide that the days we have left will be better than the ones we have lived. Believe that the God we serve can improve the rest of our days and give us back all the years that the locusts devoured, as mentioned in Joel 2:25. Therefore, we should never lose faith. Many people have lost faith and never entered God's plan for their lives. Some never achieved anything in life and lost everything they had. The rest destroyed their families and were abandoned by the people they relied on. Some died because they missed several opportunities to escape a situation that jeopardized their lives. They saw the threat but persevered on this path of bewilderment because they thought they were strong. They convinced themselves they would rise victorious from this situation, but instead of rising, they, unfortunately, fell and died.

Others decided to kill for their freedom, and today, they find themselves in prison. This would never have happened if they had fled. Beloved, let's not be one of those. Let us have the courage to recognize that things are not going well. If they go from bad to worse, it is better to leave than to cling to a semblance of happiness. No one can change a man; only God can. Do not carry burdens that endanger our lives and prevent us from experiencing peace and happiness. A wise man sees the threat and flees. Don't think God will protect us when He asks us to flee. When we find ourselves in situations where we know we cannot resist sin or temptation or no longer feel safe, running is better than staying and wasting our lives. It is better to flee than to succumb to temptation. Joseph fled from the wife of his master Potiphar because he did not want to sin against his God. He would instead go to jail than disobey God.

In contrast, King David knew that watching Uri's wife with envy could lead him to sin. Unlike Joseph, he did not run away from temptation. He stayed in the palace instead of going to the battlefield, and unfortunately, he not only succumbed to temptation but also killed Uri. This did not please God, and David was punished severely. King David confessed his sin, and the Lord restored him. We are indeed children of Almighty God, and He can get us out of any situation. He can deliver us from the hand of our oppressors because *the hand of the Lord is not too short to save, nor His ear too dull to hear*" (Isaiah 59:1). However, that does not prevent him in certain circumstances of life from asking us to flee.

Running away becomes the only way to save our lives and protect us against the fiery darts of our oppressors. God spared the lives of many of His servants by telling them to flee. Fleeing should not be seen as a sign of weakness but rather as a protective strategy by God to save our lives and get us out of danger. Therefore, when God asks us to flee, we must obey Him immediately without trying to reason. As we said above, some people will hesitate to think: 'The Lord has taken me out of this situation, He will certainly take me out of this'; or 'This situation is no worse than the time I was in'; or 'when I almost died during such an attack.' It's true, the Lord has already protected you, and you did not need to escape. This is all true as the present situation seems less severe than last time.

Beloved, we are not leading the fight, but the Lord is the one who fights for us. The battles are different, and the combat strategies are never the same, for the good and simple reason that if your opponent understands that you never change your strategy and that you always fight him in the same way, be sure that he will study your method and will eventually defeat you. The Lord is the general of our army; He is in a better position to know how our adversaries operate. Therefore, let us trust Him by submitting to His orders. If He recommends us to flee during a fight, then let's not disobey; let's flee. The Bible says that *"the horse is made ready for the day of battle, but deliverance belongs to the Lord"* (Proverbs 21:31). We fasted, prayed, and wept before the face of the Lord, imploring Him to help us get out of this situation that troubles us. He answered us by asking us to flee. Let's not reason anymore. Let us obey His command because *the Eternal will fight for us, and we just need to be still* (Exodus 14:14).

Let's take the example of King David. He beat lions and bears to death when shearing his father's sheep. The Lord saved him *"from the clutches of the lion and the* bear" (1 Samuel 17:37). The Lord also gave him victory against Goliath, the giant. As he says himself: *"The Lord does not need a sword, nor a spear to give victory. He is the master of war"* (1 Samuel 17:47). However, the many victories of King David against the lion, the bear, Goliath as well as all the successes he achieved during his military expeditions when he was in command of the troops of King Saul, all these feats that he accomplished did not stop him from fleeing when King Saul threatened him to death.

If your life has no value to you, it won't have value for anyone else. It is our responsibility to take care of the life God has given us. This life is only well protected in the hands of the Lord. It is true that it will not be easy and will require much courage and that sometimes we can encounter adversity on our path. Trouble can come from people around us or ourselves with feelings like fear of tomorrow and starting all over again. All this is normal, but you must know how to take risks in life. If Moses had remained in the palace with the pharaoh, God would have never chosen him to deliver the people of Israel from the slavery they suffered in Egypt. Even better, Moses would never have had conversations with God.

The Bible says, in Exodus 33:3, that *"The Lord spoke with Moses face to face as a man speaks with his friend."* Moses had a privilege that no man before, during, and after him would ever have. However, Moses needed to flee far from the Pharaoh and live in the land of Midian to have such a privilege and accomplish the plan God had for him. This plan was to deliver the people of Israel from bondage. Another example is that of Joseph. If he had succumbed to the advances of Potiphar's wife, he would have never become Egypt's prime minister. The only person who was above Joseph in Egypt was the pharaoh. Joseph was only thirty when Pharaoh gave him authority over all of Egypt. He would never have become Prime Minister if he had not fled the house of his master Potiphar because it was after his escape that he was thrown into prison. It is because he was in this prison, following his escape, that the pharaoh could give the order to go and find him so that he could interpret his dreams.

God can do for us what He did for Joseph. He is the One who changes times and circumstances. Let's have faith and take courage; let's have no regrets because the best is yet to come. Nothing to regret because we were not happy, which is why we ran away from this place. Let's not look back during our escape. If we have any regrets and decide to return to the home of bondage, our life will never change. Regrets, remorse, and murmurings are potent obstacles to change. Because of these attitudes, we may go around in circles and accomplish nothing in life. We accept suffering, hoping for a better tomorrow.

Beloved, you must learn to choose good over evil, even when it hurts, and no one supports you. Indeed, the primary support we need is that of God. The Bible tells us that: *If God is for us, who can be against us?* (Romans 8:31). So let's understand that we are already in the majority alone with God. Regrets, false hopes, or always remembering the past will not achieve anything. This kind of attitude will never allow us to move forward.

On the contrary, it will stand in the way of our march toward a better future. The past is past, and the best is never in the past; it is always to come. When you live in regrets and the past, your life is limited, and you block your future. God has given us the capacity to overcome the sad and painful situations of the past. If the heroes of faith could do it, we too can overcome this situation; we can cross this desert and emerge victorious.

Let us never be limited in life because the God we serve has no limits. The only limitation of God is us because the Lord will always act in our life according to our faith. We can no longer change our past, but our future is full of opportunities. So, let's act like apostle Paul; *let's do one thing: let's forget what is behind and stretch forward, let's press on towards the goal to win the prize for which God has called us heavenward in Chris Jesus.* (Philippians 3:13-14)

It's time to move on and give meaning to our lives.

The time has come to write a new chapter in our lives, and this is only possible if we forget the past and focus on the future. Let's arm ourselves with courage and be persevering and consistent in our effort without ever looking back. The Lord Jesus Christ said, *"No one who puts his hands to the plow and looks back is fit for service in the Kingdom of God"* (Luke 9:61). If we want to be of service to the Kingdom of God, we must learn to move forward and be focused on our goal, paying no attention to any form of distraction. This is the attitude the Lord wants us to have during our escape. Distraction must not be in our escape; otherwise, we will miss the point. The journey initially supposed to last a week, or a few months can turn into several years. Regrets are a distraction that can lead to our loss during the journey. Indeed, pursuing the path of freedom is not easy, especially after years of bondage or suffering. Therefore, we must keep faith in God and make Him our guide in our walk toward our freedom.

By fleeing, our faith will be strengthened, and we will find the strength not to be discouraged and not to give up. However, those who will have regrets will see that they will not be able to achieve anything in life. They will live in the hope of a better tomorrow which unfortunately will always be uncertain because their hope is not based on God but on their feelings. But the Word of God declares, *"Except the Lord builds the house, their builders labor in vain"* (Psalm 127:1). This verse means that there is no hope and safety apart from

God. Building something or fighting against a situation is only possible with the support of the Lord. Anything that is not supported by God always ends up falling apart. It may last longer, but it is only temporary because the real wealth is spiritual, the type that gives us eternal life through faith in Jesus Christ.

We make too many wasted efforts in life for the love of the world, people, and things of this world. Ultimately, we will have regrets, feeling like a statue because our life will have just stood still. If We don't move, we can't accomplish anything in life, and our situation will go from bad to worse. In that case, we must understand that we have become slaves to our misery. We no longer have power over our problem, but our problem controls us. This is how we end up paying the price for our regrets. This is what happened to Lot's wife.

Lot's wife certainly looked back because she heard the destruction of Sodom and Gomorrah. This noise confused her mind and distracted her. She looked back and disobeyed the Lord, who had told them not to look back as they fled. Many of us act like Lot's wife. Indeed, people may call us during our escape; some will need explanations, and others will judge us. Even those who hurt us will try to convince us they have changed. We are going to lose many friends. Some people will even distance themselves and consider we are no longer frequentable. Our friends will line up with our enemies to destroy us. Others will say that our escape will end in failure and that we will come to beg them to take us back because, for them, we cannot get by without them. When we have reached our place of refuge, these sounds of the past will pursue us. Our persecutors will send us threats and use everything to destroy us in our place of refuge.

For those who fled with a child, don't be surprised if your oppressor fights to get the child or children back. Be aware that his motive is not the love of these children but an ardent desire to make you suffer by separating you from them. If this happens, be strong and recommend your children into the hands of the Lord so that He protects them every day and every night. This prayer should be your daily life. Ask God for divine protection over your children so no misfortune befalls them. Also, ask Him to give you His peace so that *"your hearts will not be troubled, nor be alarmed"* about your children. (John 14:27)

God is faithful; He will protect them, and no matter how long, these children will return to you one day. I know it's difficult, but sometimes we must leave our children behind in certain situations. In most cases, people flee with their children. However, don't beat yourself up if you can't do it. Know that your children should have a living father or mother far from them than a dead or unhappy parent beside them. It is traumatic for a child to see his mother being humiliated or beaten daily by his father. This is so painful that it will affect their future life negatively.

People will fuss around us to scare us. However, whatever noise we hear as we flee, let's not look back. Even though it's hard, we must stand firm, asking the Lord to strengthen us daily. Let us cling to the word of God; He will be our strength and support. The Lord who brought us out of bondage will watch over our children and us. It is He who has chosen this place for us, a place where we will be safe. He has a plan of peace and happiness for us in this place. Therefore, let us remain faithful to Him and never forget our condition in the past, how the Lord delivered us from it, and how He made us flee to save our lives.

If we flee for our lives, it means turning back or looking back will destroy us and cause our death, the death that those who made us suffer want to see. The reason God asks us to flee is simply that He loves us and wants our happiness. Isn't He the One who said: *"I know the plans I have made for you, plans of peace and not of misfortune, to give you a future and hope"* (Jeremiah 29:11). In this verse, we see that the word "plans" is plural. This means that the Lord has many plans for us, plans that will give us a future and hope. If we refuse to flee and always live in the past, we will never know a happy future. By making the past an important part of our present, namely our daily life, we will never achieve anything concrete in our life, and instead of having a future and hope, we will have a present and a future filled with fears, doubts, and despair.

Above all, let's not try to justify ourselves or reason when we have tried everything with our strength, and it came to nothing. It is useless to insist. You must know how to introspect, look the truth in the face, dare to take your destiny into your own hands, and get up and fight. Don't be one of those who think they came to earth to accompany others. Refuse to submit to things and circumstances by deciding to act. With the help of the Lord, nothing is impossible. Those who choose to flee for their lives have realized their value and know the destiny attached to their lives. These people are not just anyone; they are God's chosen ones who will never end their lives in the shadows. They leave a mark on Earth by impacting the lives of as many people as possible. They are doing the thing God sent them on earth for. They are heroes of faith. When He orders us to flee, the Lord will give us the reason why we are escaping as well as specific recommendations as mentioned in the book of Genesis chapter 19, verse 17: *"Flee to save your life; don't look back"* (Don't look back on the possessions you have acquired in the past and don't be distracted by the murmurings of those around you or by the "what will people say)."

Don't look back. Be the architect of your own life; forget the past and all that it contains; the best is yet to come); *do not linger anywhere in the region.* Sometimes you must move out of your town or even your country if possible. Do not waste your time by taking refuge with friends or relatives close to the place of your suffering. Get away from all these people; you need to change your surroundings. There are many hypocrites among them; in this moment of escape, you will know who your true friends are. Some of them will link up with your enemies to harm you); and most importantly, don't let anyone know about your plan to flee. Don't sound the trumpet when you are going to flee, do it in secret. Be careful, as those who resent you will take measures against you. Above all, avoid anyone directly or indirectly related to your oppressors or enemies. Do not make any noise around you; *"but commit your fate to the Lord, put your trust in Him, and He will help you"* (Psalm 37:5). He is the One who makes plans succeed, the scriptures say: *Commit your works to the Lord, and your plans will succeed. (Psalms* 16:3)

Running away is not something you should take lightly because your life depends on it, so only the Eternal by His mighty hand can help you make this project a success. *Take refuge in the mountains if you want to stay alive.* The mountain here represents a place of safety. God chose this location to shelter us from danger. It is also where we will be as far as possible from those who are after us. No one can hurt us anymore; in the mountains, we are delivered from all forms of addiction, and no evil can reach us because the blood of Jesus Christ will have purified us of all our past marks. Old things will have passed away, all things will have become new, and all fear will be banished from our lives. We will hear the noise our enemies will make. Still, we will be above them, and they will no longer be able to reach us because on our mountain of refuge, *"the Lord is with us like a mighty hero; that is why our persecutors are tottering and will not have the upper hand; they will be filled with confusion for not having succeeded: it will be an eternal shame that will not be forgotten.* (Jeremiah 20:11)

On the mountain, when we lower our heads to look at those who persecuted us, they have become tiny in our eyes and will no longer be able to do anything against us. On the mountain, the Lord will show us all the blessings He has planned for us; He will show us the whole expanse of the country with all its opportunities. We will be so blessed on the mountain that we will even forget the sufferings of the past. We have walked through our desert and come out victorious because we have chosen to trust in the Lord regardless of the obstacles encountered while crossing that desert. Now that we are out of danger, we are opening a new chapter: entering fully into God's plan. God saved us from danger because He has a specific plan for us, and He wants us to be able to accomplish the plans He has for us.

Dear Ana,

"Run for your life, don't look back; don't linger in the
234

area; take refuge in the mountains if you want to stay alive." (Genesis 19:17)

"Don't be afraid now because I am with you. Do not be dismayed, for I am your God. I will strengthen you and help you; I will uphold you with my righteous right hand. All who rage against you will surely be ashamed and disgraced; those who oppose you will be as nothing and perish. Though you search for your enemies, you will not find them. Those who wage war against you will be as nothing at all. For I am the Lord your God who takes hold of your right hand and says to you, do not fear, I will help you." (Isaiah 41:10-13)

I know it won't be easy, but you must run if you want to save your life. Therefore, rely on this word that I have given you and be courageous and strong: *"Let this book of the law not depart from your mouth; meditate on it day and night, to act faithfully according to all that is written therein; because it is then that you will be successful in your undertakings, it is then that you will succeed. Did I not give you this order: Strengthen yourself and take courage? Do not be afraid or dismayed, for I, the Lord your God, am with you wherever you go (Joshua 1:8).* So, arm yourself with courage and strength because in fleeing, your adversaries will begin to pursue you, *"they will wage war against you, but they will not defeat you; for I am with you to deliver you (Jeremiah 1:19).* However, when you arrive at your place of refuge, peace, and prosperity, *"Be careful not to forget the Lord by failing to keep his commandments." (Deuteronomy 8:11)*

"Be careful not to become so proud to the point of forgetting that the Lord your God brought you out of the house of slavery... He made you encounter difficulties to humble you and test you, so that in the end, it might cause you to prosper. Never think that you have achieved prosperity by your own strength. Remember that it is the Lord your God who gives you the strength you need to achieve this prosperity." (Deuteronomy 8:14, 16-18)

May the Lord keep you and protect you throughout your life, and may He open a wide path before you and your offspring. I repeat to you one more time: be strong, take courage, and always remember that whatever adversity you will face, *"the sufferings of this present time are not worth comparing with the glory that is to be revealed to us." (Romans 8:18)*

Ana may the peace of the Lord be with you, and may the Lord bless you and your son, may He cover you with His divine protection and may happiness and grace accompany you all the days of your life.

Continuation of the story:

On October 31, 2013, my son and I got visas to enter the United States. Two days later, my little sister

Larissa, who has been living in the United States since 2005, booked plane tickets for us online and sent me the flight information.

Departure date: November 16, 2013
Departure time: 4 p.m.
Airline: Delta Airlines

Why did you choose this date? Quite simply because it was the birthday of the person I was running away from and whom I suspected of having organized a romantic weekend with his beloved. I was correct; he went to the station on November 16 at 5 am to take his train to Seoul. It was not in my interest to meet him while trying to escape. I decided to take the bus to get to the airport a bit earlier. We drove 4 hours from Dong Daegu Station to Incheon International Airport.

I had been fasting and praying for more than 40 days. I was sleeping on the floor in my son's room. I took only our important documents and threw away all the rest of my belongings. I had to be highly vigilant. The passports were under the mattress of the matrimonial bed. There was no better hiding place than this place. Apart from my sister Larissa, my two aunts Charlotte and Georgette in the United States, and my close friends Julie and Ange in South Korea, no one else knew of my escape. My son didn't know about my plan because I didn't want to take any chances. He and his dad thought we did not get the US entry visa. I had never been so scared in my entire life!

It was the most significant risk I had ever taken. I was so afraid that my plan would fail. I give glory to God, who has been with me all along the way. I encountered no obstacles during my flight. When our plane landed at Fort Worth International Airport in Dallas, I realized that my past was far behind me and that it was a one-way trip. While we were waiting for our next flight to Washington DC, I took my son's hand and began to pray, thanking the Lord for this new door He had just opened in my life and, above all, for having supported and strengthened me during all the hardships I had gone through. I knew that many trials still awaited me. However, I kept my faith and trusted in the Lord. I knew He would always be with me and never leave me. I was convinced of one thing: that I would never look back and that I would never have regrets.

Today on my mountain, God gave me something I didn't have. This is his peace, which I wanted to keep at all costs and that I didn't want to lose for anything in the world because it was a gift from God. I could now sleep fearlessly as my past was behind me, and I could now walk confidently on this new path with my best friend, Jesus Christ, by my side. I ended this book by talking about my escape to encourage all people going through difficult times, particularly women who are victims of domestic violence.

Beloved, I know this is hard; you have already tried everything to escape this situation without success, and now you are discouraged and have lost hope. I want to tell you this: with God, it is never too late, and know that *the hand of the Lord is not too short to save, nor His ear too dull to hear* (Isaiah 59:1). God is not insensitive to your situation. Keep crying out to Him until He brings you out of this trial. If you must run, then run and don't look back. Value your life and have faith in God. Do not be discouraged; be strong, even when deliverance lingers to come. Keep hope. Know that with God, it will undoubtedly happen. And sometimes, this deliverance is called running away.

Several women have lost their lives because of domestic violence, don't be next on the list; your life is precious in the Eyes of God. If you die today, you may never have the chance to fulfill God's plan for your life, you will not see your children grow up, and your dreams will never come to pass. The church will certainly judge you but know that it is not the members of the church who endure your suffering, much less your family, friends, and acquaintances. Stop keeping silent in faith and despair when your life is in danger. You must save your life! The Bible says, "*God so loved the world that He gave His only begotten Son, that whoever believes in Him should not perish but have everlasting life.*" (John 3:16)

My sister, the situation you are in now is killing you, and before you know it, you will lose your life and salvation. Before your faith can be used to save your neighbor, it must first save yourself. A lost soul cannot save anyone. It's time to leave this place that destroys your life and makes your marriage look harmful to your kids. God's blessing is never followed by sorrow; if this marriage or this relationship causes you distress, makes you live in fear, without peace, in humiliation and suffering, if you are a victim of domestic violence, if your life and that of your children is in danger: Run for your life!

You can't do anything alone; turn to the Lord, and He will do it. If He did it for me and many before me, if He is doing it now for others, beloved, know that He will certainly do it for you. Have faith in Him, for only He can change your situation. Be strong in His word and take courage; even in your place of refuge, your enemies may still attempt to harm you. It is then necessary to be courageous and anchored in the Word. Nothing is easy in this world. I speak to you knowingly. My adversary had set out to pursue me, and his plan to harm my life was well calculated. The pain he had put me through before was nothing compared to what he intended to put me through. I now understood why every time I opened my Bible, I always came across the verse that said: *"Be strong and take courage."*

My story was beginning. The story of a life transformed

by the mighty hand of the Lord Jesus Christ. Today, seven years later, we are precisely January 29, 2020, in Chevy Chase, in the State of Maryland in the United States, where I have become a permanent resident. My divorce was finalized in February 2016, and I live alone as I lost custody of my son, who only spent ten months in the United States with me.

Don't feel sorry for me because God has dried my tears, and my son is doing well with the grace of God. Since we were separated, I have never gone a single day, a single hour, not even a second, without thinking of him and praying for him, asking the Lord to protect him and take care of him. I thank the Lord for the peace He has given me so that I have no worries about my son. It's not easy, but as a Fang proverb (an ethnic group located in the north of Gabon, a country in Central Africa) says: "The snail's saliva follows the snail." So, it's just a matter of distance and time because no *man can separate what God has united."* God is in control.

Sometimes I wonder if I'm the one who suffered all this domestic violence and humiliation. The woman who started this book and the woman who is finishing it today are two different people. God has blessed me beyond what I could imagine or think. The irony is that the best is yet to come. Words are not enough to express all my gratitude to the Lord because He answered me from the bottom of my distress. I was looking for a solution to my distress, and Jesus Christ came to me as the Answer to my cries.

God is a good God, so I give Him all the glory, honor, and praise for what He has done and continues to do in my life. It wasn't easy, but it was worth it because I learned obedience to God through all my hardships.

To be continued...

"If you hear his voice today, don't be stubborn!"
(Hebrews 4:7)

CONTACT THE AUTHOR

Email: AkeleBooks@gmail.com

Instagram @akelebooks

Made in the USA
Middletown, DE
29 October 2023

41447803R00156